Faith-Based Policy

Faith-Based Policy

A Litmus Test for Understanding Contemporary America

John Chandler

LEXINGTON BOOKS
Lanham • Boulder • New York • Toronto • Plymouth, UK

Published by Lexington Books
A wholly owned subsidiary of Rowman & Littlefield
4501 Forbes Boulevard, Suite 200, Lanham, Maryland 20706
www.rowman.com

10 Thornbury Road, Plymouth PL6 7PP, United Kingdom

British Library Cataloguing in Publication Information Available

Library of Congress Cataloging-in-Publication Data
Chandler, John, 1954 May 16–
Faith-based policy : a litmus test for understanding contemporary America / John Chandler.
pages cm.
ISBN 978-0-7391-7902-4 (cloth : alk. paper) —ISBN 978-0-7391-7903-1 (ebook)
1. Faith-based human services—Political aspects—United States. 2. Human services—Government policy—United States. 3. White House Office of Faith-Based and Community Initiatives (U.S.) 4. United States. White House Office of Faith-Based and Neighborhood Partnerships. 5. Church and state—United States. 6. Religion and politics—United States. 7. Bush, George W. (George Walker), 1946– —Political and social views. 8. Obama, Barack—Political and social views. 9. United States—Politics and government—2001-2009. 10. United States—Politics and government—2009– I. Title.
HV530.C43 2014
361.7'50973—dc23
2013041462

Printed in the United States of America

Contents

Preface

I have resided in France since the end of the 1970s. While this piece of information might seem to be somewhat arbitrary, it does help to clarify one of the major reasons that brought me to write this book: the distance I have come to feel towards American Christianity since my departure.

This feeling of distance may be partially explained by my American experience of religion before coming to France. I was brought up in the household of a highly successful minister-church developer for the Presbyterian Church USA. And as I have come to realize, my father and his colleagues were dynamic embodiments and products of the Great Society. They were participants and partners in its utopic vision of a society where government would lead a "war" in eradicating poverty and injustice from the face of the nation. Influenced by this vision, I have always had, therefore, an instinctive belief that government should be the primary source of social aid for the needy in American society.

Inverse to the results of my up-bringing in the States, the distance I feel towards American Christianity is also, without a doubt, the result of subsequently never having had an American experience of the Reagan era, nor of the later rise of the "armies of compassion" in the 1990s. Since 2001, I have watched from afar as the expression of this compassion took form in the faith-based policy of both the Bush and Obama administrations.

It is not surprising, then, that my initial reaction to faith-based policy under the Bush administration was openly critical. However, given the persistent popularity of such policy with the American people, I became, over time, more of a detached, albeit fascinated, observer. In attempting to understand and explain the multi-faceted importance of a consistently popular policy, I came to see how, for example, its development under Bush and Obama serves as a litmus test for understanding new values and new paradigms that are reshaping American society. I also became aware that analysis of Obama's approach to his oft-criticized faith-based policy provides insight into the beliefs and actions of the president and his administration. At the same time, I progressively realized that in the polarizing debate which invariably accompanied this policy, the religious theory behind it was, for the most part, very poorly understood and represented. The possibility of my being useful in elaborating an impartial, "distanced" exploration of these different facets of faith-based policy contributed greatly towards my undertaking this study.

Acknowledgments

I would like to thank those who aided in the elaboration of this work, whether through granting me their precious time in interviews or through editing and commenting on my analysis. In particular, I would like to thank Michael Gerson and Richard Mouw for the time they spent with me in discussing the subject of this study. I would equally like to extend the same thanks to John Dilulio, who also read part of the text and contributed written commentary (as well as some very good food). I am very grateful to my friend and colleague, David Coad, for the help he gladly supplied during the editing process, while another friend, Christopher Adde, has my thanks for his help in creating an unbelievable work environment at the Huntington Library. Special thanks go to Jack Rogers, who, from the beginning of this project to its completion, provided me with invaluable commentary, general encouragement, and friendship. Finally, I am indebted to Stanley Carlson-Thies for his, quite simply, astounding generosity. Throughout this project, Stanley Carlson-Thies consistently demonstrated a willingness to discuss, comment, and, generally contribute invaluable insight, even when he wasn't necessarily sympathetic to the arguments being advanced. As the French would say, *"un grand merci."*

ONE

The Need to Know

In the early years of this millennium, American society became increasingly characterized as being subject to, and divided by, a cultural war. George W. Bush, of course, did not initiate hostilities, but only intensified a polarization of the electorate that had become evident[1] in the 1980s with the alliance between conservative, evangelical Christians and Republicans. Though the simplified reality of a culture war was considered by many to be reductive and exaggerated (Kemeny 29), it is clear that the popular perception was nevertheless one of a pitched battle between two camps. And in this process of "dueling for values" (Gergen 58), morality and religion progressively came under the monopoly of the Republican Party, while the Democrats were correspondingly relegated to an increasingly narrowed identification as secular.

With its red state, blue state Union, the 2004 presidential election combined with the media's "revelation" of the American voter's preoccupation with moral values to fuel this perception of contemporary America (Reed 2–3). As Dan Balz underlined, the battle for the presidency between George W. Bush and Democrat John Kerry only served to buttress what was perceived as a growing cultural divide and chasm between the Democrats and the Republicans[2]: "Political polarization intensified during the 2004 elections continuing a trend that has defined voting behaviour for most of the past decade and that has left the two major parties increasingly homogenized and partisan" (A4). Confirming this viewpoint, other analysts[3] drew attention to voting statistics that underlined how American voters were increasingly aligning themselves into two camps.[4]

It may then come as a surprise that during this period of increasing animosity, one of the Bush administration's most controversial instruments for change introduced in 2001, the Faith-Based and Community

1

Initiatives, continuously enjoyed the support of the vast majority of Americans (formally known as the Faith-Based and Community Initiatives, the initiatives and the policy behind them are commonly and more generally referred to as, simply, the faith-based initiative). From the moment George Bush signed two executive orders in 2001 creating the White House Office of Faith-Based and Community Initiatives and other subsidiary offices within a number of government departments, the support spanning his two administrations consistently hovered around 64 to70 percent.

The driving force behind the initiative was to create a "level playing field" where faith-based organizations could compete on an equal footing with secular organizations for government funding of social aid programs. With the anticipation that such programs would be involved in "curbing crime, conquering addiction, strengthening families and neighborhoods, and overcoming poverty" (Exec. Order No. 13199, 2001, Sec.1), the federal government was attempting to encourage and support faith-based participation from a wide range of organizations. Bush thus extended legal principles of the Charitable Choice provisions written into the 1996 Personal Responsibility and Work Opportunity Reconciliation Act introduced during the Clinton administration.

Faced with the continuous decline of the Bush Administration's popularity after the 2004 presidential elections,[5] questions arise then concerning the origin and foundation of this sustained pro-faith majority. Staunch defender of the Bush administration, and former head of the White House Office of Faith-Based and Community Initiatives, John Towey asserted that

> President Bush's faith-based and community initiative is deeply rooted in America's heartland. . . . It's established; it will continue to bear fruit for years and years to come. And I thank God for President Bush's leadership on an initiative that has faced a steady headwind from day one ("Towey Leaving" 14).

It is true that Towey's contentions were attacked on many different fronts. One of the most vocal critics of the initiative, the executive director of Americans United, Rev. Barry W. Lynn, challenged Towey's interpretation, noting that faith-based policy was essentially moved forward through executive orders signed by Bush and that "the president [had] yet to persuade Congress to pass a comprehensive faith-based bill" (Leaming 16). Furthermore, Lynn also accused Towey and the Bush Administration of using the faith-based grants for political ends and not for the needy: "Towey played a key role in using the 'faith-based' initiative for improper partisan purposes, and he did little or nothing to see that Americans get the social-service help they need from their government. That's a sad legacy to leave" (Leaming 16). However, faced with all these observations and accusations concerning partisan politics, political foul play and the absence of legislative ratification, it is all the more striking that even towards the end of Bush's mandate (in August, 2008), faith-based policy was in some form or another still supported by 67 percent of the American public. In other words, as Lew Daly comments in *God and the Welfare State*, the faith-based initiative seemed to "take us beyond the culture war and the entrenched church-state positions of the day" (xviii–xix). And it seems clear that Bush did somehow introduce and apply policy which struck a responsive chord in a vast majority of Americans.

This feeling was reinforced when, despite the obvious multiple short-comings of faith-based policy under Bush, Barack Obama repeatedly de-clared in the 2008 presidential campaign his desire to not only continue, but to "elevate the program to a 'moral center' of his administration" (Zeleny and Knowlton). To the surprise of many, and to the consterna-tion of some liberals, this pledge did not prove to be just a political ploy to gain votes. On the contrary, the commitment of the new president to this controversial approach to faith in government and social aid became apparent in the creation of his Office of Faith-Based and Neighborhood Partnerships. Moreover, as was widely diffused by the general press,[6] with volatile situations both at home and abroad greeting the new presi-dent on his arrival in office, one of Obama's first priorities was to set up his faith-based office. In carrying forward the effort to help faith-based organizations acquire public funding, it is also noteworthy that Obama's office gained in influence, being charged with such tasks as facilitating interfaith dialogue, more responsible fatherhood and fewer abortions.

Given, on the one hand, this continuation of faith-based policy and, on the other, the continued support by the vast majority of the American people for some form of faith-based policy, the need for self-examination emerges concerning the course of action that religious organizations should take. How should they meet this expectation by the public? Whether a faith-based organization plans on ever using government funding is only part of the question. Just as important is the necessity to understand and to meet responsibly the demands of one's culture. Con-sequently, any faith-based organization should have a position concern-ing such policy. In the same way, the citizen, whether fearful or not of such policy, should clearly understand what it is and the issues that it raises. Why? First, because whoever comes after Obama, it is highly doubtful that any subsequent president would seriously consider taking on the dissolution of the Office. In other words, despite the apprehension of an evangelical like Richard Mouw,[7] or the reserve of a Barry Lynn, this doesn't seem to be a policy that is likely to just go away. Secondly, it is also a policy which has set and is setting precedents that with time will only become more entrenched and accepted in the institutional fabric of American government and culture. And if it won't go away, then, how should responsible policy be conducted?

While the present book responds to this need to understand, it also acknowledges that there is already a substantial amount of documentation available, which, taken together, provides a comprehensive picture of faith-based policy.[8] My general objective is to contribute a relatively brief, accessible analysis that draws on and synthesizes the available information. More specifically, I will concentrate on providing insight into: 1) the theological visions of the faith-based actors behind the policy; 2) how these actors have tried to apply these visions as the program has evolved in the 2000s; 3) the divisiveness and debate that has characterized the faith-based experiment, and; 4) how all of the above may be held up for contemplation by the reader as a mirror of developing American culture.

This leads to a certain number of details concerning the method and organization of the book. First, wishing to give the reader the most representative information in a reduced amount of space, choice of material will be oriented by its illustrative capacity and efficiency. For example, in discussion of the religious theory and its application in the Bush initiatives, I will highlight the Calvinist, Protestant theory of sphere sovereignty (or its contemporary expression, principled pluralism) more than the Catholic theory of subsidiarity. I will also, in particular, focus on the Center for Public Justice as a case study. One reason for this is because of the undeniably key role principled pluralists played, especially from the small yet potent CPJ, as catalysts in the effort behind the creation and initial application of the Bush administration's policy.[9] However, equally as important is the subsequent reality that the Bush administration (and faith-based policy) will increasingly be identified as being subject to a theocratic, evangelical Dominionism that is far more extreme than anything envisioned by the principled pluralists. As this extreme evangelical perspective has a greater affinity with the Calvinistic roots of principled pluralism than with subsidiarity, the Protestant vision is also accentuated in order to better delineate the wanderings of a drifting Bush administration.

Secondly, the story of faith-based policy is one which comprehends different forms of pluralism, whether it be religious (or confessional), cultural, structural, or political. While referencing this multi-faceted term, my focus is nevertheless on illustrating how the diverse thought behind the policy has ultimately translated into political perspectives concerning the way authority may (or may not) be legitimately attributed to groups in government.

Thirdly, the presentation of the study is chronological, tracing the interlaced story of the policy from the theory behind its inception to its present-day expression in the Obama presidency. Indeed, faith-based policy today and the challenges it faces cannot be understood without knowing the story behind it. And as we will see, while Americans have an opinion about faith-based policy, they in fact seem to know very little about where it originated or what the theory behind it actually has meant and means today.

Fourthly, in order to accomplish the above-mentioned synthesis, this study remains neutral and takes no side in the controversy surrounding the policy.

Finally, in the effort of providing a relatively brief, accessible text, there is a substantial amount of information (about 20 percent of the text) in endnotes, available for the reader wishing greater detail.

In response to the objectives of this study, the second chapter, "Finding an Instrument of the Spirit—European Roots," confronts the question of how and why the policy may be poorly understood. In attempting to make sense of the confusion surrounding the policy my analysis takes as its point of departure Lew Daly's sound council that the theological history behind the faith-based initiative is "worth studying" (*God and Welfare* xviii). Chapter 2 consequently provides a brief background for understanding the initiative by concentrating on the most influential visions behind its inception, the neo-Calvinist political theory of sphere sovereignty (or principled pluralism as it is now termed) and its Catholic counterpart, subsidiarity. Here I will also underline the differences between the two in order to show the roots of disagreement that will subsequently be expressed in relation to application of the policy.

The third chapter, "The Roots Take Hold in the United States," traces the conditions which led to an American need to appeal to such new and different doctrines as subsidiarity and principled pluralism. In particular, we will see how certain American thinkers took issue with the tenets of the Enlightenment and progressivism. Disillusioned with the enormity of the tragedies and disappointments of the twentieth century, they reacted to the pretensions of such doctrine by taking aim at the belief in, as Reinhold Niebuhr termed, an "immanent logos" that was seen as unfolding in secular history and where the perfectibility of man through science and reason was fully attainable.

Here we will feature theoreticians who specifically sought alternatives for governance through a pluralistic distribution of authority that took into far greater account the formative role of associational and social groupings (religious included) in society. Details concerning the characteristics of the pluralism of these thinkers will also be set off against the background of the pluralism of American behavioralism and the inherent dangers of interest group politics. Facets of the otherness of this pluralism from the American model will then be further defined in an evaluation of how the theory behind the Bush policy corresponds to traditional political party-line identification and to conventional political theories differentiating left-right approaches to government's role in social aid. These considerations also lead to the assertion that the principled pluralist is inherently more inflexible about delegating power to a centralized government, and consequently more militant about his/her belief system, than the Catholic. I might also add that this contributes to my reasoning in highlighting the modern-day torch-bearers of the Protestant theory as reference points for understanding where the Bush policy came from and what it was supposed to be.

After a discussion essentially oriented by the theory behind Bush's faith-based initiatives, the fourth chapter, "The Context for Growth in the New Millennium," briefly frames the policy within the wider conditions impacting the initiatives' introduction. For example, I trace the progressive desecularisation of American government (or, inversely, the deprivatisation of religion) through Charitable Choice and the role of the American judiciary system. Against these positive developments for faith-based backers, the more negative circumstances against which the new policy was perceived are also illustrated, such as the growing economic stratification of American society and the fear of the devolution of government into a negative connotation of governance. With the above information established as a backdrop, one of the major points of this short chapter is to demonstrate and underscore the need on the part of the Bush administration for a reassuring clarity of purpose and intent. This chapter thus acts as a preface for understanding the fall-out for faith-based policy issuing from an administration that subsequently failed in coherently communicating the policy to the American people.

Moving on from the establishment of a general background for understanding theory, chapter 5, "From Theory to Application—Conflicting Signals," focuses more precisely, then, on the theory as it was expressed in the Bush faith-based initiatives. At the same time, this chapter explores how the identity of Bush's policy became subject to a tangled mix of Christian messages forwarded by different actors that were assumed to be part of the same team effort. To demonstrate the misunderstanding of the theory our analysis: 1) centers on the introductory phase of the faith-based policy under the Bush administration; 2) showcases the principled pluralist organization, The Center for Public Justice, in order to delineate the guidelines that were intended to define the Bush faith-based initiatives, and; 3) inversely uses "the father of compassionate conservatism," Marvin Olasky, in order to clarify how these guidelines came to be misinterpreted and misunderstood in subsequent criticism of the policy. Both visions can be argued to have played, in their respective ways, a formative role in the way faith-based policy was expressed. Both visions also designate roles for religious organizations in ways that would have been inconceivable two decades ago. Yet a comparative analysis enables the reader to have not only a clear understanding of the conflicting lines of thought that often categorized faith-based policy, but also of the relative dangers inherent in each.

Chapter 6 also makes use of two reference points in order to illustrate and orient our study of the Bush administration's failure to apply the policy. Entitled "Theory in Application—Conflicting Use of the Instrument," this chapter concentrates on, first of all, 9/11 and its impact on the faith-based agenda, and secondly, the trajectory of John DiIulio, the first Director of the White House Faith-based Office. If underlining the importance of 9/11 might seem an obvious choice for providing insight into Bush's subsequent approach to policy, I highlight the unique case of DiIulio as I consider his particular role and his particular perspective (that of a Catholic and a Democrat) as excellent and revealing vehicles for illustrating both the chain of events leading up to 9/11 and the fall-out that 9/11 had on faith-based policy. Moreover, the Catholic DiIulio serves as a filter for our summarizing conclusions concerning the Bush administration's faith-based effort as well as key characteristics of American support.

After considering the Bush era, my analysis moves on to evaluate how and why Obama has been trying to transform such policy into what he considers a coherent and efficient "foundation [for] a new project of American renewal." Specifically, chapters 7 and 8 constitute a response to Stephen Mansfield's injunction that Barack Obama's "faith is not only sincere, but also the most important thing about him: it is impossible to understand who he is and how he will lead without first understanding the religious vision that informs his life . . . and there can be no shrinking from the political implications of his faith" (xxiii). Both chapters seek to penetrate the religious thinking behind Obama's quest to create a coherent response to the faith-based legacy that was left him.

Chapter 7, "New Theory—Obama and Lessons from Life," provides the first of two phases of analysis concerning Obama's religious vision. Here we will illustrate the salient facets of Obama's faith through a short biographical analysis that centers on his experience at Trinity Church, in South Chicago. A first objective here is to establish the basis for evaluating how Obama's particular brand of pluralism corresponds to the legacy of religious social theory behind Bush's faith-based policy. A contingent objective is to evaluate how his faith may be considered consistent with the objective of bringing the American people back from the alienation and extremism of the Bush era to a more consensual middle-of-the-road policy.

Chapter 8, "New Theory—Obama, Niebuhr and Liberals," continues the outline of the theory behind Obama's brand of faith-based policy by placing particular emphasis on the thought of Reinhold Niebuhr. This analysis responds, first of all, to the growing literature affirming the importance that Niebuhr has for Obama. However, beyond the influence on Obama, Niebuhr's vision is also held up to be of potentially widespread importance, both as a contemporary guide to government for faith-minded American liberals, as well as a counter-weight to the right's claim on all that is religious and moral. The analysis in chapter 8 responds to and complements chapter 3, where we discuss theory that provided avenues of thought for the more Conservative Christian. In general, we might note that chapters 7 and 8 respectively add to descriptions of Obama which affirm that he represents in his persona a unique synthesis that offers the potential for profound transformations in American culture.

Chapter 9, "Theory in Application—A New Partnership with Americans?," squarely places the Obama administration in the evolving saga of applied faith-based policy. Reflecting the study of Obama's "theory," analysis here evaluates how the president's program simultaneously addresses the heritage of the Bush administration while constituting a project for the future. Here we evaluate how the response to these challenges translates into a vigorous policy that seeks to develop new, but non-controversial avenues for program expansion such as the development of civic (and not just financial) partnerships with faith-based organizations and the implementation of policy goals in order to give direction to the partnerships.

Likewise, we consider in this chapter how the lack of accountability and transparency that came to stigmatize the Bush program will be addressed by a spectacular and unique illustration of theory in practice—the creation of the President's Advisory Council on Faith-Based and Neighborhood Partnerships. Indeed, in its make-up and its influential role in providing direction to the president, this multi-faceted tool serves as an excellent reflection of Obama's brand of confessional, cultural, and political pluralism. Finally, we will assess the success of the Obama effort in light of an on-going and defining problem that has plagued faith-based policy since the Bush era, the religious hiring issue. Throughout the chapter, we will particularly reference what Stanley Carlson-Thies rightly described as an impressive means for summarizing "past and present policy," the December 17 conference at the Brookings Institution, "Four More Years for the White House Office of Faith-based and Neighborhood Partnerships."

After discussion of what the policy reveals about those involved in its creation, I evaluate the meaning of the policy within the wider framework of the American people at large. With this objective, the concluding chapter, "Obama, Faith-based Policy, and 'the Center,'" uses as references: 1) the latest actor in the faith-based story, Barack Obama; 2) Jack Rogers's assertion in his 1995 book, *Claiming the Center*, that, "most modern Americans are neither conservative nor liberal . . . [but] clustered somewhere in the center" (xvi), and; 3) the question of whether Rogers's assertion has, after the polarization of the Bush years, any renewed value with Obama and, if so, what the "center" signifies. Faith-based policy will be analyzed, therefore, within the context of how Obama's presidency may be seen as reflecting tendencies from across the political spectrum (and not just for liberals of faith who want to put religion back into their conversation). In short, after the Bush years, Obama's attempt at representing a more middle-of-the-road America serves as a prism for focusing contemporary currents of American religiosity.

NOTES

1. Although the usual understanding of this period is one in which an aggressive and militant coalition between neo-conservatives and the Religious Right took over the reins of the Republican Party, certain argue that this was a reaction to the previous secularization of the Democratic Party and its policy in the 1960s. In other words, the roots of a "culture war" predate the Reagan era.

2. Balz added that "The findings came as no surprise to election experts but as confirmation of patterns that now appear ingrained in American politics" (A4).

3. Mark Gersh of the National Committee for an Effective Congress, an organization that provides Democrats with analysis and advice about congressional and presidential voting patterns, further affirmed "that the parties are ideologically more homogenous than they used to be and more active in partisan activities all the time, rather than just closer to the election" (A4). For a short, concise analysis concerning religious aspects of the "ideology," see John C. Green, "Winning Numbers," *Christian Century* 30 Nov. 2004: 8.

4. This had increasingly been the case since the mid-1990s. In the 2004 presidential elections, "93 percent of self-identified Republicans backed Bush and 89 percent of Democrats supported Kerry. Independents went 49 percent for Kerry and 48 percent for Bush. In 2000, there were 86 such 'split-ticket' districts, and in 1992 and 1996, there were more than 100 such districts. In 2004 Bush won 255 congressional districts to Kerry's 180. More strikingly, Bush tallied 214 districts held by congressional Republicans and 41 districts that were won by Democratic House candidates. On the contrary, Kerry only won 18 of the districts that are Republican" (Balz A4).

5. According to the CNN-USA Today-Gallup poll taken just after the presidential election (on November 22), 55 percent of Americans liked the way President Bush was handling his job ("CNN-USA"). Less than a year later 42 percent of the people (Connelly and Toner A1) said they approved of the way Mr. Bush was handling his job: "[This constitutes] a marked decline from his 51 percent rating after the November election, when he embarked on an ambitious second term agenda led by the overhaul of Social Security" (Connelly and Toner A1). By April 20, 2006, President Bush's approval rate hovered at 33 percent ("Poll: Gloomy").

6. *U.S. News and World Report*, for example, advanced that the creation of Obama's faith-based office and his creation of the Advisory Board constituted two of the "top ten faith moments" in Obama's first, vaunted, 100 days ("Ten Most").

7. In an interview, Mouw (who beyond being a noted theologian was president of Fuller Seminary until May, 2013, the largest evangelical seminary in the world) told me that the question of a religious organization's right to hire along religious lines might present an insurmountable obstacle. The subject of religious hiring will be a recurrent theme in this study (Personal interview 28 Oct. 2012).

8. Notably, for an understanding of the movement of faith-based policy through government before and during the Bush presidency, see Amy Black, Douglas L. Koopman, and David K. Ryden's *Of Little Faith: The Politics of George W. Bush's Faith-Based Initiatives* (Washington D.C.: Georgetown University Press, 2004). For a concise overview of the theology which enters into the Bush policy, see Lew Daly's *God and the Welfare State* (Cambridge Mass. and London: The MIT Press, 2006) or Daly's *God's Economy: Faith-Based Initiatives and the Caring State* (Chicago: University of Chicago Press, 2009). For insight into the positions of major denominations, see P.C. Kemeny's (Ed.) *Church, State and Public Justice: Five Views* (Downer's Grove: InterVarsity Press, 2007). For more general studies which affirm that faith-based policy is a reasonable, historically appropriate, middle-of-the-road policy for the United States, see: Stanley Carlson-Thies and Dave Donaldson's *A Revolution of Compassion: Faith-Based Groups as Full Partners in Fighting America's Social Problems* (Grand Rapids, Mich.: Baker, 2004); John J. Dilulio Jr.'s *Godly Republic: A Centrist Blueprint for America's Faith-based Future* (Berkeley: University of California Press, 2007); E.J. Dionne Jr.'s *Souled Out: Reclaiming Faith and Politics after the Religious Right* (Princeton: Princeton University Press, 2008);

Jim Wallis's *The Great Awakening: Seven Ways to Change the World—Reviving Faith and Politics* (New York: HarperCollins, 2008) or Wallis's *Rediscovering Values: On Wall Street, Main Street and Your Street* (New York: Howard Books, 2010). For arguments against faith-based policy see: Susan George's *Hijacking America: How the Religious and Secular Right Changed What Americans Think* (Cambridge, U.K.: Polity Press, 2009); Barry Lynn's *Piety and Politics: The Right-wing Assault on Religious Freedom* (New York: Three Rivers Press, 2007) or; Garry Wills' *Head and Heart* (New York: Penguin Press, 2007). To discern more clearly the faith of Barack Obama and what it has brought to the above policy see Stephen Mansfield's general biographical portrait in *The Faith of Barack Obama* (Nashville: Thomas Nelson, 2008). R. Ward Holder and Peter B. Josephson provide an extremely useful and comprehensive theoretical analysis in *The Irony of Barack Obama: Barack Obama and Reinhold Niebuhr and the Problem of Christian Statecraft* (Farnham, U.K.: Ashgate, 2012). In the more general context of Obama's brand of government, see James T. Kloppenberg's intellectual biography, *Reading Obama* (Princeton: Princeton University Press, 2011).

9. For a brief, yet concise description of this role, see Daly's *God and the Welfare State*, Chapter 6, "The Makings of a Movement," 59–73.

TWO

Finding an Instrument of the Spirit: European Roots

Investigating the instruments available to the Bush administration for the creation of the faith-based initiative leads us to first see that it takes from late–nineteenth-century Protestant and Catholic doctrine. Resulting from the conflict pitting European Christians against liberals and socialists, the doctrine subsequently rose into the form of European Christian Democracy[1] and, after World War II, was extensively applied as Christian Democrats took the reins of government power in numerous European countries. Exploration of the formative role that such a doctrine played in contemporary America necessitates a very brief survey of its roots, which are to be found in the Catholic social theory of subsidiarity and the Protestant equivalent, sphere sovereignty.

In the case of Protestant thought, sphere sovereignty is a late-nineteenth-century social theory originating with the Calvinist theologian and Dutch prime minister, Abraham Kuyper.[2] More specifically, as a reflection on the creation of the privately funded Free University of Amsterdam[3] in 1880, Kuyper outlined in the inaugural address a vision in which the sovereignty of spheres "stands in the first place for freedom for civil society organizations from excessive government rule over life (education is a sphere with its own norms, not a department of the state) and, secondarily, for freedom from secular uniformity" (Carlson-Thies "Comments").

In a June 8, 1877, editorial in *De Standaard*, Kuyper had already provided the following tenets for what would become his own particular brand of pluralism:

> 1) The idea that people decide what is normative in life (called popular sovereignty) is opposed to the Word of God, which teaches that God is

11

sovereign as the final lawgiver; 2) Christians confess the relevance of
God's Word even for politics, rejecting a vague concept of natural law
or human reason; 3) The office of the state has been ordained to be
God's minister for justice through the conscience of public officials who
believe in his ordinances; 4) Educational responsibility rests with parents and not with the state. The idea that, for financial reasons, Christian people have only a secularist public school open to them must be
rejected. (qtd. in Daly *God and Welfare* 46-47)

Behind these tenets, we first of all see that Kuyper refutes the Enlightenment pretentions where: 1) reason is held up to be the ultimate standard
of perfection and; 2) politics or the state are (or may be) conceived as
functioning independently of God. Secondly, the tenets express, reciprocally, Kuyper's belief that there is an organic, natural social order which
is grounded on divinely defined structures, or spheres, where each "has
its own identity, its own unique task, its own God-given prerogatives. On
each God has conferred its own peculiar right of existence and reason for
existence" (qtd. in Spykman 167). And it is within this vision that society
is considered as being constituted by "social groups, related organically,
rather than of individuals related impersonally" (Jellema 482). Thirdly,
we are witness to how, within this vision of a natural order, spheres enjoy
both a theological and a moral priority over the state. As Stephen Monsma notes, they are considered as existing "prior to and in a real sense
independently of the state" (*Positive Neutrality* 145). Finally, as underlined in the third and fourth tenets, we see in the power allotted to the
state that Kuyper's intention was to "counter the idea that such entities as
the state or the family . . . exist only because the state grants them the
right to exist. Governments do not *grant* these rights; they are called to
reorganize rights. We have families and churches and economic systems
because they are grounded in creation itself" (Mouw *Abraham* 24). While,
as Daly observes, sphere sovereignty thus assigns "a public purpose to
religious organizations" (*God and Welfare* 8), government is invested with
the duty of coordinating and maintaining equilibrium within this larger
natural order.

In general, we have seen, then, that Kuyper's emphasis on the inherently indispensable role played by collective groupings such as charitable
organizations, the church, and the family leads to a vision of humanity
where "it is so constituted that the individual can exist only within the
group and can come to full expression only in community" (Kuyper qtd.
in Spykman 187). Moreover, in this community of spheres,[4] the collective
groupings are considered to be as natural and as defining as the individual:

Human life . . . represents an infinitely composite organism . . . Call the
parts of this great instrument cogwheels, each driven around its own
axle by its own power; or call them spheres, each field with its own
exciting life spirit—the concept or imagery does not matter—as long as

you acknowledged that there are all kinds of spheres in life. (Kuyper qtd. in Spykman 188)

Based on Kuyper's anti-individualism (as well as on his anti-statism), modern-day Kuyperians therefore affirm the fundamental role of groups, associations, and communities in the functioning of a society. And this assertion of the social nature of human beings compels contemporary followers to oppose individualism (at least in its extreme forms) while the emphasis on structural, confessional, and political pluralism compels them to also oppose collectivism and totalitarianism.

Contemporary Kuyperians also insist that sphere sovereignty requires principled pluralism, in which there is "a society of self-governing religious differences protected and supported by the state" (Daly *God and Welfare* 56). More particularly, the tenets found in theologian James Skillen's[5] following definition of the term can be clearly seen as extensions of those discussed in relation to Kuyper's editorial:

- [Principled pluralism first] means recognizing that the state itself is but one institution community among others in society. The American republic, as a political community, is part of a diverse social landscape . . .[6]
- Governments may not ignore or displace other kinds of human responsibility in other institutions. Pluralism also means, therefore, that government should recognize and uphold the diverse organizational structure of civil society . . .[7]
- "Principled pluralism" means that government is obligated to do justice to society's non-governmental organizations and institutions as a matter of principle . . .
- Finally, pluralism means that there should be constitutional recognition and protection of religious life in society. Principled pluralism means that government should give equal treatment to different communities of faith . . . Therefore, government should not try to establish one religion or to enforce secularism in public life. ("What Distinguishes")

It is perhaps not surprising that in this vision of cultural self-governance, contemporary Kuyperians such as Skillen now call themselves "principled pluralists" and "see a kind of organic order without hierarchy, where the autonomy of the parts ensures the order of the whole" (Daly *God and Welfare* 56).

We can note that this vision has been influential in Reformed Christianity circles in the United States since the early twentieth century. It also has correlates in the United Kingdom, in large part due to the thinking of a group known as the English pluralists who, as the twentieth century got underway, had a Kuyper-like concern with the general population's increasing acceptance of unbridled state growth.[8] More recently, and undoubtedly a result of faith-based policy, Kuyper's name and vision have become far more common in generalized conversation concerning the social gospel, social theory, and, more exactly, Catholic social theory.

The Catholic, pluralist response to the same currents of individualism and collectivism that threatened Protestants, subsidiarity, became the significant, if implicit, foundation in Catholic social thinking through Pope Leo X III's 1891 encyclical, *Rerum Novarum*. [9] This encyclical constituted a pluralistic response by the Roman Catholic Church to the increasing challenge of the collectivism and individualism represented in nineteenth-century social thought in Europe. Moreover, as Skillen and Rockne M. McCarthy point out in *Political Order and the Plural Structure of Society*, faced with the threat of both liberalism and socialism, Catholic social thought returned "with new vigor and adaptive creativity to the work of Aquinas in order to address the needs of contemporary industrializing and differentiating societies" (138). The pluralism forwarded by the church was thus based on the Thomistic precepts that social life displays many different kinds of human relationships and capabilities and that human reason is both "capable of discovering not only the natural truth and necessity of a differentiated social order but also the truth of its hierarchical structure" (McCarthy and Skillen 139). [10] While being at the top of the hierarchy in God's creation, the human being is nonetheless a social animal where each individual is subject to a social hierarchy of groups. For example, the individual is part of the family, which in turn "exists at the base of the social hierarchy which reaches its natural fullness and self-sufficiency in political community" (McCarthy and Skillen 139). In general, subsidiarity provides a pluralistic vision of the structure of society where the parts are harmonized in a higher unity.

More specifically, subsidiarity is considered to be the foundation for a body of principles and theories that have oriented the doctrine of Catholic Social Teaching. In an assessment of contemporary CST, Clarke E. Cochrane provides the following description of the most vital tenets within the doctrine and their relationship to subsidiarity:

> Most central are that government is part of the natural order of creation, that the primary purpose of government is attainment of the common good in pursuit of justice, that the condition of the poor is the principal measure of common good and justice, and that solidarity with all persons in defense of human freedom and dignity are essential principles of governance. Moreover, the state has a responsibility to maintain order in the social and in the natural world; hence, stewardship of God's generous gifts is a prime responsibility of governance. Finally, CST embraces the principle of "subsidiarity," which entails that the commitments just stated are not the exclusive domain of the central government but are the joint responsibility of governments at

all levels and of families, churches, economic enterprises and voluntary associations. (47)

Subsidiarity therefore provides an associational and organic framework for social action and, as such, we see obvious similarities between it and sphere sovereignty. However, subsidiarity may also be argued as being distinct from its Protestant equivalent in that it inherently leaves more of a place for centralized power. Daly goes so far as to warn us that the above definition is very far from the "secular, federalist version of subsidiarity enshrined in the Maastricht Treaty of the European Union" (*God and Welfare* 77)[11] where, closer to the spirit of sphere sovereignty, the term is understood as advancing a social order in which political decision-making by a central power should be avoided if at all possible.

To clearly identify the roots of this distinction between the Protestant and Catholic doctrines, Robert Benne provides a useful framework for comparing the two in his article "Christians and Government." Considering the question of how much Christians should involve themselves in political life, two categories for action are each respectively applied to the Catholic doctrine behind subsidiarity and the Calvinism behind sphere sovereignty. Subsidiarity falls within the category of what Benne terms "Christ above politics." Here Benne traces the roots of Catholic doctrine back to the thought of Aquinas where it was "reflected in the practical life of the High Middle Ages," and where there was "a grand synthesis between Christ and culture, the church and politics. It is a hierarchically ordered fusion that features one God, one son of God, one vicar of Christ on earth, one church, and one king over one kingdom. The grand unity—called Christendom—is presided over by this supernatural wisdom and grace of the church" (332). In short, above the King and the government, the Church enjoys final say in the hierarchy of authority: [the] "differentiated social order and the diversification of human tasks was the direct result . . . of the decree of Providence" (McCarthy and Skillen 139) and natural law. The result is that subsidiarity seeks to define "the harmonious relations among persons and institutions [within] a hierarchically ordered society" (McCarthy and Skillen 140). While it is true that, as Benne observes, in "the last half-century the Roman Catholic Church has distanced itself from the "Christ above Politics" model,"[12] he also notes that "the church still encourages a robust role in politics for the Catholic laity, that offers guidance to both its members and society with its social teachings" (333). The point is that subsidiarity involves a redistribution of the power of the Catholic Church that, while modifying it, does not cancel out the power of the centralized church—there is still a residual, centralized authority that remains a fundamental part of the Catholic worldview.

On the other hand, Calvinist thought belongs in the category "Christ Transforming Politics" (336). Benne observes that the Calvinist perspective towards involvement of Christians in politics was based on "creating a Christian society through politics, not one directed by a hierarchical church, but one directed by godly magistrates formed by the church. God's reign in and through worldly institutions is not something negative, but expansively positive" (336) Confident in its capacity to establish a Christian society, the Calvinist Reformation was founded on the belief that

> the Bible reveals a discernible pattern—called the 'third use of the law' in reformed theology—for holy life Christians informed by the Holy Spirit have the capacity not only to discern this pattern but to construct an approximation of the kingdom of God on earth. This constructive approximation takes place in politics, economics, culture, and social institutions. (337)

We may first see how, then, from the Calvinist approach, Catholic thinking may be considered more hierarchical:[13] " . . . in the world of practical ethics as well as in the sciences the impact of Calvinism was to drive human beings to explore and to act on the creation. This [had] a secularizing impact in the sense of undermining the Catholic Church's claim to being the chief and highest mediator between God and the world. Calvin emphasized the creation's direct dependence on God in all its dimensions" (McCarthy and Skillen 21). Inversely, we can also underline how the basis for sphere sovereignty leads Calvinists to a more individualistic worldview: "Not only is every believer a priest before God, but . . . under the impact of Calvinism human social life could become more radically differentiated and free from ecclesiastical control" (McCarthy and Skillen 21). This engendered what Richard Mouw calls a celebration of "many-ness" in Kuyperian thought that can be seen as issuing forth from the Reformation's rupturing of the unity of the church. The freedom from ecclesiastical control also leads to the consequent assertion that the true church "can reveal itself in many forms . . . in the multiplicity of institutions" (*Abraham* 16). The result is that principled pluralists today have "frequently emphasized the presence of worldviews (i.e., systems of thought that are built on fundamentally different assumptions) . . . [and] this notion of worldview is tied to the 'pluralist' component of the principled pluralist label . . ." (Smidt 73). Likewise, again to use Mouw's terms, Kuyperians see the world as one of created complexity in which "the creator [has] deliberately woven many-ness into the very fabric of creation" (*Abraham* 17). The inherent confessional and cultural pluralism that principled pluralists see in the world leads therefore to a logical and firm opposition to the Catholic notion of natural law.

In application, this theory of "worldviews" inherent in sphere sovereignty and the neo-Calvinism of principled pluralism translate into putting greater stress on the associational as opposed to the centralized and hierarchical. As a result, principled pluralists acknowledge their sympathy to subsidiarity,[14] yet argue that the Catholic doctrine "embrace[s] a more hierarchical concept of social order and the role of the state" (Daly *God and Welfare* 77) than does sphere sovereignty.[15] As Mouw cautioned, "all things considered . . . the relationship between subsidiarity and sphere sovereignty is not an exact fit" (*Challenges* 39). Understanding this divergence between subsidiarity and principled pluralism is necessary for, as we will see, it will be the groundwork and reference for later: 1) generally understanding the thought behind the faith-based initiatives of the Bush era;[16] 2) specifically understanding the positioning of faith-based actors as regards the balance of power between group and government and; 3) qualifying the American people's reaction to the policy.

NOTES

1. Originating at the end of the nineteenth century, with the Catholic Church, Christian democracy was quickly adopted by Protestants as well.

2. While Kuyper is responsible for the concept of the sphere, the model for both sphere sovereignty and subsidiarity is rooted in the revolutionary thinking of the German (and Calvinist) political philosopher Johannes Althusius (1563–1638).

3. We might note that in more recent times, influential players in the faith-based story such as James W. Skillen and Stanley Carlson-Thies studied there.

4. Richard Mouw provides more precision concerning the characteristics of the Kuyperian sphere when he defines it as "pretty much what we have in mind when we talk about a person's 'sphere of influence.' It is an area where interactions take place, and where some sort of authority is exercised" (*Abraham* 23).

5. Skillen is also former director of the Center for Public Justice.

6. Reflecting Kuyper's approach to the state as the guarantor of justice in a world of spheres, Skillen affirms that "the jurisdiction of American federal and state governments is (or should be) limited to the making, executing, and adjudicating of public laws for everyone who lives under the jurisdiction of those governments" ("What Distinguishes").

7. Again mirroring the words of Kuyper, Skillen adds that "government should not treat human beings merely as individual citizens; human beings also exist as family members, faith-community members, economically organized employers and employees, and in dozens of other capacities and relationships" ("What Distingusihes").

8. Notable among these pluralists are John Neville Figgis, G. D. H. Cole, and Harold Laski. For a comprehensive survey of the three, see Paul Hirst, Ed., *The Pluralist Theory of the State: Selected Writings of G. D. H. Cole, J. N. Figgis, and H. J. Laski* (New York: Routledge, 1993).

9. Elaborated by Oswald von Nell-Breuning, the term subsidiarity later influenced in 1931 the social thinking of Pope Pius XI as expressed in his encyclical Quadragesimo Anno. It was here that subsidiarity was explicitly defined in the context of Catholic social policy.

10. For a concise description of the Thomistic vision of the human in the natural order and how the person is a social animal, see McCarthy and Skillen, 139.

11. Daly adds that "the Community shall take action, in accordance with the principle of subsidiarity, only if and insofar as the objectives of the proposal action to not be sufficiently achieved by the member States . . ." (*God and Welfare* 77).

12. More specifically, Benne explains that "The church no longer claims to wield direct political power, though it still holds a religious value should deeply influence

political life. Popes John XXIII and John Paul II have led the church to accept liberal democracy and religious freedom" (333).

13. McCarthy and Skillen thus argue that the thinking of Calvin has a far greater affinity with the pragmatic approach of modern rationalism than with the thought of Aquinas (21).

14. For example, see Mouw, *Abraham*, 26-27.

15. For example, Daly underlines that Pius XI's 1931 encyclical refers back to *Rerum Novarum*, which promoted workplace reforms, capital-labor reconciliation, and Catholic worker organizations and thus played an important role in salvaging the church from the more antimodernist currents that favored socialism in the competition for working-class loyalty" (78). He underlines however, the 1931 document's lack of comment concerning democracy, which "foreshadows the Church's alliances with fascism in the 1920s and 1930s . . ." (78).

16. Beyond familiarizing briefly the reader with one of the most important theories behind Catholic Social Teaching, our analysis of subsidiarity is meant to set off the ideology which subsequently serves as the best illustration of the roots of faith-based policy in the Bush administration, sphere sovereignty.

THREE

The Roots Take Hold in the United States

Given this brief survey of the theoretical background of the faith-based initiatives, the question now becomes—why a recourse to such doctrines in the United States? A first answer is to be found in post–World War II disillusionment of certain American historians and analysts with the Enlightenment belief that progress is inevitably unfolding in history. Specifically, this disillusionment is, if not issuing from, at least reinforced by the reign of terror and fascism of two world wars in a supposedly enlightened Europe.[1] In 2005, Arthur Schlesinger captured this disillusionment and loss of innocence when he wrote:

> The notion of sinful man was uncomfortable for my generation. We had been brought up to believe in human innocence and even in human perfectibility. This was less a liberal delusion than an expression of an all-American DNA. Andrew Carnegie had articulated the national faith when, after acclaiming the rise of man from lower to higher forms, he declared: "Nor is there any conceivable end to his march to perfection." In 1939, Charles E. Merriam of the University of Chicago, dean of American political scientists, wrote in *The New Democracy and the New Despotism*: "There is a constant trend in human affairs toward the perfectibility of mankind. This was plainly stated at the time of the French Revolution and has been reasserted ever since that time, and with increasing plausibility." Human ignorance and unjust institutions remained the only obstacles to a more perfect world. . . . The belief in human perfectibility had not prepared us for Hitler and Stalin. The death camps and the gulags proved that men were capable of infinite depravity. The heart of man is obviously not OK (Schlesinger).

Here we are witness to what Reinhold Niebuhr termed an "imminent logos" where he saw a secularized idea of progress in which an imminent

19

order "was no longer related to a transcendent meaning, but was inherent in history itself. And this idea of progress was something that had emerged out of Christianity, that was in some sense an outgrowth of Christianity's worldview and ethos, but that had threatened to negate Christianity" (McClay "Obama's Favorite").

While Niebuhr is perhaps the greatest modern theologian to comment caustically on the "naïve" perfectibility of man, given my present purpose of focusing on the associational models behind the policy under Bush, we will briefly analyse certain assertions of a major, conservative critic of American liberalism, Robert A. Nisbet, and their pertinence to the thinking that went into the Bush project.

Confronting the depravity of WWII despots in *The Quest for Community: A Study in the Ethics of Order and Freedom* (1953), Nisbet argued that Western liberalism could provide no basis for the explanation of such evil and that the conception of history as some sort of liberating process "of man from despotism and evil" (214) is, in fact, what he denounced as a myth of the Enlightenment. In this context, belief in the Enlightenment theory of the progress of human freedom is condemned by Nisbet for leading to: 1) the disregard of all or anything that may be good or positive in traditional associational and community groupings; 2) the paradoxical result where the individual risks becoming subject to an ever-increasing bureaucratic and possibly totalitarian state (227–28). Here Nisbet advances that "the conception of society as an aggregate of morally autonomous, psychologically free, individuals . . . is, in sum, closely related to a conception of society in which all legitimate authority has been abstracted from the primary communities and vested in the single sphere of the state" (228). While it is true that a number of Nisbet's arguments are now considered dated and debatable,[2] they nonetheless seek to demonstrate how the collectivism inherent in totalitarianism and communism, and the individualism[3] inherent in much of Western liberalism "share a common root in the Enlightenment ideals of human self-sufficiency and world mastery" (McCarthy and Skillen 2).

The relevance of Nisbet's arguments to the thinking behind the faith-based policy can be seen in McCarthy and Skillen's observation that a key element in the Enlightenment conception of history is also the role of secularization: "generally speaking, both the champions and the critics of modernization assume that the 'modern world' represents a new era in history marked by its break (for better or for worse) from a medieval past . . . [and that it] is a secular world even if religion still thrives here and there . . ." (19). Nisbet's post-war arguments and the above observation help to clarify, then, how recourse to the religious social theories of subsidiarity and sphere sovereignty could be seen as providing alternative theoretical frameworks for analysts who, rejecting certain Enlightenment tenets as exposed falsehoods, fear at the same time the potential alienating (and terrifying) individualistic and collectivist extremes that they affirm such tenets can engender.

In general, the above arguments curiously bring to mind those of postmodern analysts, for they are essentially evaluating the same question as to why there should be any acceptance of the Enlightenment assertion that human consciousness is the ultimate measure of truth and goodness. However, unlike the postmodernists, principled pluralists like McCarthy and Skillen, for example, do not accept that there is no meta-narrative. Consider that after asking if the secularization of the world is nothing more than an empty declaration made by a passing ideological voice, they immediately refer to the sociologist, Max Weber, the American legal scholar Harold Berman, and others who, respectively, find the roots of modern capitalism or the Western legal tradition in some form of Christianity.[4] Note that McCarthy and Skillen are obviously aware that, for example, some of Weber's views are no longer held to be tenable. Nonetheless, it is clear that in citing such research (whether it be more or less recent) they are countering postmodernist declarations and Enlightenment dogma with the suggestion that the roots of the modern world can equally be argued as being grounded in Christianity.

Building on the above framework, a further explanation as to why such models as subsidiarity and sphere sovereignty have found their way and been funnelled into Bush's faith-based policy again finds its roots in rejection and disillusionment. Here, of course, we are talking about reactions which took place after a loss of faith in the promise of the Great Society and New Deal government, and the subsequent, dizzying swing to the right with Reagan and the neo-conservatism of the 80s.

The swing was set into movement in the 1970s with, as a backdrop, the continued loss of influence of mainline denominations, the rise of a heretofore marginalized religious right made up of fundamentalists and evangelicals,[5] and the increasingly central role of, as Kenneth White labelled them, values politics. James Davison Hunter advances that two contradictory poles of thought, one progressive, the other Orthodox were increasingly alienating the American people. Cutting across denominational divides, these rallying points posited an either-or situation as far as the question of a moral authority and a contingent worldview were concerned: on the one hand there was recourse to an external "transcendent" authority for the orthodox camp, while for the progressive camp, moral authority was to be found in "the spirit of the modern age, a spirit of rationalism and subjectivism" (Hunter 44). And Hunter goes so far as to affirm that every facet of American life was in some form subject to this increasingly alienating cultural war between a religious right and a liberal left. While it is true that the extent of this allegedly all-encompassing acrimony may be debated, it remains that as the United States advanced towards the 1980s, it was becoming progressively clear for all to see that on many battlefields the War on Poverty was not being won. Sensing the failure of the Great Society as an illustration of the dangers stemming from a society in which the state has increasingly appropriated all legitimate authority (at the expense of other spheres), certain writers (generally categorized within the framework of what became known as compassionate conservatism) attempted to go beyond a reactionary libertarianism and to elaborate what they advanced as more responsible alternatives.

A prime example is the neo-conservative Peter Berger who, in his earlier career, was part of the vast majority of sociologists that were predicting the inevitable secularization of the world. Moved by what he considered to be unmistakable proof to the contrary (the continued prevalence and even growth of religion), Berger sought other approaches. Specifically, he drew the wrath of more confirmed liberals when, on the one hand, he argued that there was an exponential multiplication of bureaucratic programs and resultant interest groups through which the power of the individual was increasingly being delegated. And on the other hand, he equally aroused ire when he came out for the empowering of "mediating structures"[6] that are on the ground level with communities such as voluntary and neighborhood associations, churches, and the family.

Later, in 1984, conservative Christian Richard John Neuhaus, provided another major cornerstone in alternative theory with the publication of his *The Naked Public Square: Religion and Democracy in America.* Here Neuhaus erects and inscribes a legal reference point for the subsequent application of theory to practice through the courts by attacking what he argued to be a secularizing, strict-separationist interpretation of the First Amendment. This interpretation is not only "the result of political doctrine and practice that would exclude religion and religiously grounded values from the conduct of public business," (ix) but also one, affirms Neuhaus, which leads to hostility towards religion (which is, paradoxically, proscribed by the First Amendment). The result is a "naked public square" stripped of both religious expression and legality. Neuhaus argues therefore for the rightful return and need of the presence and voice of mediating structures like religious groups in public debate and decision making.

What in fact Neuhaus did was to orient and spark what would become an intense movement for what is called the neutrality interpretation of the First Amendment. This is also called the equal treatment or equal protection doctrine. This perspective is opposed to what is often termed the doctrine of separationism. Its relationship to the question of faith-based social aid policy is summed up by Dave Donaldson and Stanley Carlson-Thies in their book, *A Revolution of Compassion*:

> No-aid separationism told government to try to be fair to all faiths by excluding them from all government support. The result was discrimi-

nation against faith-based programs and organization. The new "equal treatment" strategy instead requires government to be even-handed . . . If equal treatment was the right way to interpret the First Amendment's twin requirements to promote religious freedom while avoiding establishment of religion, then it was time for a new guideline for government funding of social services provided by other organizations. (48–49)

This will be the legal foundation for the argument that it is unconstitutional to deprive religious providers of social aid of government funding on the unique grounds that they are religious.[7]

At approximately the same time as Neuhaus was taking on the First Amendment, other writers such as Michael Walzer[8] were contributing more theoretical arguments that attempted to ground the necessity of the sovereignty of spheres[9] in history for the successful pluralistic dispensing of justice by a government in a complex and differentiated society. Walter's objective was to develop "an argument from history to the effect that government in a complex society should not try to become the sole distributor of all social goods, and certainly should not try to do it so simply by means of interest-group politics" (McCarthy and Skillen 9). In short, as Walzer's recommendations highlight, we see in the thinking leading up to Bush's faith-based project that it is perhaps a simplification to affirm that only compassionate conservatives from the religious right like Neuhaus or Berger express both a preoccupation with "spheres" and a professed antagonism towards interest-group domination.

What is also of particular interest to note in relation to these thinkers, though, is the argued differentiation between the pluralism of such advocates as Walzer with the pluralism of American behavioralism. This latter understanding of pluralism has a highly negative connotation that dates back to debate in the early 1960s. Here the question of what constituted the nature of domestic American political power pitted, most notably, C. Wright Mills against Robert A. Dahl. In his classic, *The Power Elite*, Mills denounced the American democratic system as a manipulative illusion where power was concentrated in an elite social group representing financial, military, and political interests. Representing the pluralist perspective in his classic, *Who Governs?*, Dahl attacks the pretention that in a democracy there can be the homogeneity that Mills advanced as unifying one decision-making group composed of "an elite." For Dahl, democracy in America is held to be a polyarchy, based on a battle for political power that is fought by competing interest groups of individuals who are essentially interested in nothing other than their own particular interest(s).

According to the pluralist point of view stemming out of subsidiarity and sphere sovereignty, the basis of the conception that American behavioralists have of groups is to be found, in fact, in the Enlightenment tradition of individual autonomy. For example, McCarthy and Skillen provide the following explanation:

[G]roups are functional organizations of individual interests. There is
little if anything in the writing of these scholars that points to a pluralistic philosophy of institutional and associational differences derived
from qualities and characteristics unique to each unity. Group behavior
theory is an attempt to provide an empirical explanation of political
interest group activity; it is not a philosophy of social pluralism . . .
Dahl [and others] . . . use pluralism simply to describe certain power-
balancing functions performed in the liberal society. (5)

Unlike the American behavioralists, therefore, the theoreticians we have
been studying posit a type of pluralism that seeks norms and structure
that, comprehending the essential necessity of groups or mediating structures, enable a society to avoid individualism and collectivism. Pluralists
like Nisbet, Berger, Neuhaus, and Walzer, are argued as calling into question, each in his respective manner,

> simplistic ideals of individual autonomy, liberation from all traditional
> authorities, and an egalitarian society of individuals maintained
> through a process of interest group politics. They point, in essence, to
> the emptiness of a freedom ideal that promises to liberate individuals
> from all such obligations except the universal and ubiquitous demo-
> cratic ones. (McCarthy and Skillen 10) [10]

Defining justice as being the recognition of group, as well as individual
rights, this brand of pluralism is thus a social philosophy and a directive.
The primary concern of its advocates is to find (through theory based on
subsidiarity, sphere sovereignty and ultimately principled pluralism), the
language capable of coherently categorizing "the structural differences
among the diverse institutions and associations of society" (McCarthy
and Skillen 5).

    This evaluation of the thought of a Nisbet, Berger, Neuhaus, or a
Walzer in the light of American behavioralism leads to a further clarification concerning the "American-ness" of the pluralism that we have been
studying. In fact, Daly's statement that faith-based policy "takes us beyond the culture war and the entrenched church-state positions of the
day," also applies to traditional party lines held by both the Republicans
and the Democrats. To find political parties that issue from the thinking
behind today's faith-based policy, one must rather look to those who
constitute the Christian Democratic parties, particularly in Europe. [11]

    When thinking of Christian Democrats, most Americans have heard
such names as Konrald Adenauer, Angela Merkel, Lech Wałęsa, or Ruud
Lubbers, and perhaps know that Christian Democrats constitute the preeminent conservative power in countries such as Germany, Spain, Bel-
gium, and Holland. However, few have knowledge of who Christian
Democrats really are, and much less of what typifies their thinking concerning welfare. It is noteworthy, then, that while the Christian Democrats were rising to play a central and widespread role in much of post-

war Europe, [12] their conception of a welfare system was based not only on the rejection of the threatening collectivism they saw in prewar socialism, but also on the traditional American model which,

> typically tied health, retirement, and other benefits to employment and left the needs of the unemployed to public welfare system. Christian Democratic states featured limited state control of social services yet social spending levels roughly as high as in social democratic systems, and even higher in some cases. (Daly *God and Welfare* 24)

In other words, while being generally considered at least moderately conservative in their own counties, Christian Democrats hold tenets that represent challenges to entrenched right-wing/left-wing positions in the United States. For example, they generally are conservative on moral issues such as abortion, the role of the family, and the place that religion holds in a society, while they are also for universal health care, a strong social safety net, and state-run, low-cost education (including at a university level). In short, such positions do not really fit the traditional niches of the left/right, Democrat/Republican debate and in a very real sense they are "other."

One way to reconsider how this otherness relates to the American context is to situate the two religious social theories, subsidiarity and principled pluralism, within the more conventional theories often used in defining the left-right social aid debate, the institutional as opposed to the residual approach to welfare. Harold Wilensky and Charles Lebeaux develop this opposition in *Industrial Society and Social Welfare.*

Briefly, the residual position is anti-statist, and attributes ultimate responsibility for the safety net of the individual from the bottom up. The personal context of the individual defines the source of care, whether it be the family, various groups, religious organizations, or the economic well-being offered by a market economy through employment. It is only when one or more of these avenues fail, and that such failure is beyond the individual's responsibility, that the state offers assistance. Furthermore, aid is minimal, requires evidence of need, and only given until one or both of the other avenues of primary assistance can resume their role as caretaker. The assumption is that the individual can find the means of assistance within his personal and work life. Finally, inherent in the residual perspective is that welfare programs and policies basically respond to problems caused by individual personal failure. Inherent also is that programs are reactive and solve problems only after their occurrence.

The institutional concept of welfare is based on the premise that there is an inevitable social cost that comes with the risks of operating an industrialized capitalist market. Individuals, therefore, should not have to pay that cost and social welfare programs should protect them. The assumption is that it is neither reasonable, nor normal to assume that individuals can solve all their problems on their own and that such problems go far beyond their responsibility. Also inherent in this approach is that need, in and of itself, justifies aid. The conditions creating need are therefore not a consideration. Also, given that need for assistance is an inevitable bi-product of the market, there is no shame involved when seeking aid. This defined the liberal perspective from the New Deal, through Johnson's Great Society and up to the Reagan revolution.

Both subsidiarity and principled pluralism take the position that "poverty stems from different causes and thus people are poor for different reasons . . . [and that] poverty has a moral and personal root that public funding is unable to address" (Kemeny 152). In short the reasons for poverty vary from individual to individual and, it would seem, consequently, that both subsidiarity and principled pluralism are, without distinction, part of the residual category. Moreover, this certainly seems the case when one reads the rhetoric, espoused by the likes of Congressman Dan Coats, calling for the "inner-transformation" and the "remoralisation" of America that accompanied the arrival of Bush's initiatives. Nonetheless, this perspective is rather reductive, given that the extent of the (re)appropriation of formative responsibility at the level of individual, family, and associational life is argued, as we have seen, to differ between the two religious social theories.

In transposing the two religious social theories of principled pluralism and subsidiarity into government policy, it is therefore more exact to say that they both are more or less oriented by the residual pole. In the case of the principled pluralist perspective, based on the more individualistic Calvinist vision, adherence to the residual pole would theoretically be greater than that of the more hierarchical subsidiarity approach. The latter would at least have inherent characteristics, then, that in application would leave more possibility of maneuver as regards the institutional pole, thus allowing for more state control. In other words, if we return to the traditional grounds for Democrat/Republican social debate, it would theoretically be (far) more difficult for a strict principled pluralist to fit into the Democratic mold than for a Catholic formed within the school of subsidiarity. And this leads us to a further observation.

As we have mentioned, subsidiarity is seen by principled pluralists as embracing a more hierarchical concept of social order and the role of the state than does sphere sovereignty. This ultimately helps to explain why the latter (principled pluralism) may have played a more militant, central and leading role in making these doctrines become a reality in the Bush administration's policy.

Specifically in the American application, principled pluralism is argued as responding more precisely to traditional/historical defining attributes of American identity than subsidiarity.[13] Mouw, for example, compares the two doctrines within the context of an upward/downward delegation of power: "Subsidiarity has a tendency to delegate downwards from a central hierarchy/authority. In other words, if the higher power, if the central power cannot carry out a certain function it falls to the subsidiary, lower social group. Principled pluralism, like the traditional American delegation of power, delegates upward from the base" (Personal interview 28 Oct. 2012). In Robert Benne's general description of Calvinism, we have already seen its placement within the category of "Christ Transforming Politics." Notice that Benne's analysis continues with the description of "a robust Christianity that has, in the United States, been both institutionally and individually involved in political life.[14] It has expended great energy in transformation projects—abolition, prohibition, women's suffrage, unionization, and similar rights, among many others" (337).

Principled pluralists argue that they have been driven to fight for the removal of what they consider biased and unfair public policies and attitudes that prevent religious organizations from this possibility of participating in public life (in partnership with government).[15] In the words of the man who provided the how-to guide for application of faith-based policy in the Bush administration,[16] principled pluralist Stanley Carlson-Thies, it was they who, from the 1980s on, were "no longer content to take that which was given or 'handed down,' and who, consequently, took a lead role in making a stand and demanding (and not asking) that rights be returned to the base" (Personal interview 26 Oct. 2012).

However, it certainly can be argued that, for example, Richard John Neuhaus, the pioneer behind the attack on "the naked public Christian Democratic square" and in creating a level playing field for faith-based organizations, illustrates in his person both Catholic and Protestant involvement in translating social theories based on the doctrines of subsidiarity and principled pluralism into American policy. Indeed, originally a Lutheran, Neuhaus became a Catholic six years after the publication of his landmark book, *The Naked Public Square*. Also later when Bush became president it is clear that Neuhaus had influence in the Oval Office concerning such issues as stem cell research, abortion, and marriage.[17] Taken together, the multi-faceted influence of Neuhaus helps us understand why Wilfred McClay asserts that he is the only recent theologian who could have anywhere near the importance of Reinhold Niebuhr (considered by McClay to be the most influential theologian of the twentieth century) ("Obama's Favorite").[18] We should also be clear that other figures that were not of the Calvinist, principled pluralist camp played key roles in the initial application of the theory within the Bush White House, notably the first Director of the White House Office, Catholic John Dilulio. In general, organizations such as The Catholic Action League as well as individual Catholics (and Democrats) like E.J. Dionne equally illustrate the many voices that have been long-standing and eloquent advocates for a greater role for faith-based organizations in social aid.

Whether Americans at large, or Catholics specifically, might therefore argue about the influences that contributed to putting religion back in the public square, it is perhaps useful as a reminder to reiterate the reasons (already detailed in the introduction) for concentrating on principled pluralism. In the general interest of efficiency, it is first because of the acknowledged dynamic role the principled pluralist faction[19] had in the creation[20] and initial application of the Bush administration's policy.[21] For the same reason, I focus on the Center for Public Justice as a case study. Indeed, in the period leading up to the Bush presidency, the Center counted among its active members, Carl Esbeck, the originator of the legal framework (the grounds of which are debated to this day) used for transforming and implementing a religious social theory into a secular application, James Skillen, and Stanley Carlson-Thies. And finally, it is worth repeating that the evangelical extremism that will come to characterize the Bush administration has a greater affinity with the Calvinistic roots of principled pluralism than with subsidiarity. The Protestant vision serves to thus illustrate "the wanderings of a drifting Bush administration away from its original theoretical moorings."

NOTES

1. This same disillusionment led to the already-mentioned rise of numerous Christian Democratic governments in post–World War II Europe.
2. For a concise critique of the theories of Nisbet's arguments (where *the Quest for Community* is considered "too much the product of its time s to be a timeless classic"), see Alan Wolf's "Remembering Alienation." *newrepublic.com*. New Republic. 9 Sept. 2010. Web. 11 Aug. 2011. http://www.newrepublic.com/book/review/remembering-alienation-nisbet-community-wolfe#
3. McCarthy and Skillen call this the "ideology of autonomous individual freedom" (2).
4. For more detail, see McCarthy and Skillen, 19.
5. See, for example, Robert Wuthnow's landmark book, *The Restructuring of American Religion: Society and Faith since World War II* (Princeton: Princeton University Press, 1988).
6. For more information, see Peter L. Berger and Richard John Neuhaus, *To Empower People: The Role of Mediating Structures and Public Policy* (Washington, D.C.: American Enterprise Institute, 1977).
7. Beyond receiving no funding, another expression of "discrimination" was the common practice of religious organization of creating ancillary secular corporations or organizations in order to be able to qualify for government money.
8. See, for example, Michael Walzer's, *Spheres of Justice: A Defense of Pluralism and Equality* (New York: Basic Books, 1983).
9. I do not use the term sphere sovereignty as Walzer was not a principled pluralist. Nonetheless, Kent A. Van Til observes that "These two thinkers [Kuyper and Walzer], almost exactly one hundred years apart, use similar language to address similar issues. Both fear that the state may wield improper control over other spheres. Both recognize that each social sphere requires its own particular and appropriate norm, and that injustice will likely result when the integrity of one sphere is compromised by the intrusion of another. They seem an unlikely pair: Kuyper was a man of the nineteenth century and Walzer of the twentieth; Kuyper was a vigorous Calvinist

and Walzer is a non-practicing Jew; Kuyper was a Dutch prime minister and Walzer is an American democratic socialist and academician. Both, however, seek a political passageway that navigates between the poles of a radical individualism and an all-encompassing state. Thus, both propose pluralistic systems of justice that acknowledge diverse types of institutions and communities within pluralistic societies. Both are convinced that other political theories derived from rights from either the state or the individual alone are inadequate. Finally, both even use the same term—spheres as a construct to legitimate moral claims made in specific areas of life. The Justice of the Spheres" (268–69).

10. They also advance "the importance of a limited state that is constrained in part by its recognition of the boundaries of other social spheres, and by clear standards of justice" (McCarthy and Skillen 10).

11. Note also that Christian Democracy plays a role in Latin America (for example, the president of Mexico until Nov. 30, 2012, was a Christian Democrat). At the same time, under the influence of liberation theology, Latin American Christian Democracy is usually more progressive than its European counterpart. The conservatism/moderate conservatism of European Christian Democracy is far closer to the ideology behind faith-based policy as it has surfaced in the United States.

12. As with the perspective of Nisbet, but on a wider scale, this is a result of the fear in many European nations of the totalitarianism and collectivism that led to World War II.

13. Daly observes that "the vision of the state according to sphere sovereignty has received greater attention as far as updating and redefining is concerned than has subsidiarity" (130). Of note, though, a very useful analysis of Catholic thinking specifically in relation to principled pluralism is found in Clark E. Cochran's "Life on the Border: A Catholic Perspective." *Church, State, and Public Justice: Five Views* (Ed. P.C. Kemeny. Downer's Grove: Inter Varsity Press, 2007) 39–66.

14. Notice also, however, that woman's suffrage became progressively tied to the Purity Crusade and the defense of WASP culture against the threat of immigration and blacks as the nineteenth century closed. In other words, this robust power is not without blemish and its exercise demands close scrutiny.

15. It should be underlined that the appeal of the principled pluralist is to create a "level playing field" and not to return to some presumed, previous predominance of Christianity. Carlson-Thies notes that "The key push was to get rid of wrongful/ unconstitutional governmental restraints, rather than to guarantee that government funds would flow to religious organizations" ("Comments").

16. Arthur Farnsley remarks that Carlson-Thies "literally wrote the book on implementation of [the faith-based initiative], providing guidelines currently used by prospective faith-based contractors around the country" (29).

17. For more information, see "Bushism Made Catholic," *Time Magazine*, Feb. 5, 2005.

18. And McClay added in 2009 that "The mainline Protestant world today is no longer the place where Protestants go for fresh ideas" ("Obama's Favorite").

19. Protestants they are, but not definable under the category "mainline."

20. Already in 1996—an article in *The Washington Times*—"100–Year-Old Idea Inspires Proposal to Revamp Welfare: Pluralism Offers Role for Welfare" (Witham), gave a first public alert about the potential influence of sphere sovereignty on present-day welfare reform.

21. As stated in the introduction, a concise description of this role can be found in Daly's *God and the Welfare State*, Chapter 6, "The Makings of a Movement," 59–73.

FOUR

The Context for Growth in the New Millennium

To clearly identify the conditions leading up to and surrounding the implementation of the theory behind Bush's faith-based policy, it is first necessary to situate such theory in the wider perspective of a progressive desecularisation or "deprivatisation of religion."[1] Returning again to Neuhaus, we have seen how he was a reference for the argument against those (Strict Separationists) who maintain that "the establishment clause of the First Amendment prohibits any promotion of religion, even in a non-preferential fashion, the consequence of which is that the state promotes non-religion over religion" (Smith 151). In fact, faith-based organizations had been getting federal money for more than a century. At the same time, even at times of great funding, such as during Johnson's Great Society, there was no coherent system, nor was there any collective effort to promote the participation of faith-based organizations in public/private partnerships. This piecemeal approach was replaced with the 1996 Personal Responsibility and Work Opportunity Reconciliation Act (the Welfare Reform Act, or the Ashcroft Bill) during the Clinton administration.

In general, this act took head-on the thinking that had been prevalent since the new Deal concerning the provision of a social safety net. In a welfare-to-work program that was intent on instilling accountability into the mix, recipients were required not only to actively search for employment, but were also subject to time limits concerning the search process and contingent welfare assistance. Specifically, the provision of the welfare reform legislation that became known as Charitable Choice "required that, whenever states contract with agencies in the private sector to offer support services for welfare recipients, faith-based organizations must be eligible to compete for these contracts" (Orr). The particular nature of the program, rather than the agency was to serve as the basis of assessment. Evaluation of any program, religious or secular, had to be based on its efficiency at meeting a specific task or tasks, such as child-care or job training.

The Charitable Choice provision of the Act is what Bush's Initiatives were based on. Dilulio underlines subsequent provisions that bridged the period between the 1996 Act and the advent of the Bush administration: A second charitable choice provision was added to the Community Services block grant program when it was reauthorized in 1998. In 2000, a third charitable choice provision was added to the Substance Abuse Prevention and Treatment block grant, and a fourth one was added to the Projects for Assistance in Transition from Homelessness program (*Godly* 84–85).

As Charitable Choice and the succession of following provisions indicate, there seemed to be in the period leading up to the Bush White House a general interest in broadening the role of faith-based organizations. And it is worth noting here that this general interest included Bush's adversary for the presidency, Al Gore, who also pushed during his campaign for the dramatically broadened involvement of faith-based organizations, as well as for the expansion of Charitable Choice principles beyond where they stood in 2000 within the four provisions.

We will come back to the erosion of this identification between faith-based policy and generalized, bi-partisan support in chapter 6 (and the possibility that much of the subsequent opposition in the Bush era was oriented more towards the president and his administration rather than the actual policy). It remains that it was Bush's faith-based initiative that created headlines by radically expanding the Charitable Choice provision of the Welfare Reform Act of 1996.[2] It did this by "allowing religious nonprofits to compete for certain Federal grants on the same basis as all other organizations, provided that they did not proselytize, did not use the funds for sectarian instruction and did not conduct worship services with those funds" (Dilulio "Four More Years" 56). Under Clinton, the charitable choice provision was limited in its application to essentially two programs, TANF (Temporary Aid to Needy Families) and welfare-to-work. And though not formed under the same conditions as later offices under the Bush administration, Dilulio points out that the Clinton administration nonetheless "established, really, the first Federal faith-based office at the Department of Housing and Urban Development under then Secretary Andy Cuomo" ("Four More Years" 56).

Bush applied "Charitable Choice" across the board to all government-provided services, while dedicating "more than $100 million for a program to mentor 100,000 children of prisoners and he stimulated dozens of state and local governments to establish faith-based offices of their own" (Dilulio "Four More Years" 56). Despite criticism that can be levied against the administration's handling of faith-based policy, it remains that, as Dilulio underlines, "most of those [offices] are still in existence today and many have been added over the last four years" ("Four More Years" 56). Bush's major contribution to such policy will therefore be, as Neuhaus wished, to establish and disseminate both the rules "leveling the playing field," as well as the infrastructure for subsequent extension.

Here it should also be clearly understood that a key factor behind the possibility of this progressive movement of deprivatisation concerning religion and policy was the judiciary system, in particular, the Supreme Court. More specifically, Richard Nathan, Co-Director of the Nelson Rockefeller Institute of Government, explains that "the laws and regulations leading up to and including Charitable Choice and the Faith-Based and Community Initiative were made possible by a dramatic change in the Supreme Court's interpretation of the Religion Clauses of the First Amendment" (Nathan).

This new interpretation was first of all a rejection of what is variously termed as the second disestablishment of religion, or the official establishment of secularism, which had its roots in such cases as *Everson v. Board of Education of Ewing Township*.[3] Here Supreme Court justice Hugo Black captured the spirit of the Court's attitude at that time (1947) when, invoking Thomas Jefferson, he famously stated that "The First Amendment erected a wall between church and state. That wall must be high and impregnable."[4] This establishment of secularism led to the aforementioned doctrine of no-aid separationism that, according to Carlson-Thies, simply "did not work" (Personal interview 19 Feb. 2010). Inversely, the Supreme Court's new understanding of the First Amendment is a result and reflection of the movement for the neutrality interpretation that Neuhaus championed as an approach that will work.

Secondly, the idea of there being two absolutely distinct periods (one of strict separationism and the other of strict equal treatment) is rather reductive and undermines the significance of a continuing partnership between government and faith-based organization that continued, albeit more discretely, during the supposedly well-defined period of secularism. Stephen Monsma and Christopher Soper note, for example, that

> there is . . . more than a little irony in the fact the court decided—after articulating these ringing words of strict, even absolute, church-state separation—that the First Amendment allows government to aid religious schools in the form of subsidies to transport children to them . . . [and] there is much in this early decision that typifies the Supreme Court's approach to church-state issues. (*Challenge of Pluralism* 15)

Likewise, the precise delineation of a neutrality period must also be tempered by the knowledge that the Court's decisions have been characterized as debatable and made on unclear arguments.[5] In other words, the Court's positions indicate an on-going and heated debate that has continued to characterize the faith-based conversation throughout the new millennium (as we will see when we touch on this subject again during discussion of Obama).

A further preparatory step towards understanding the wider conditions which will affect the policy is a clarification of the economic situation during the Bush era. Here we can note that at approximately the same time that Bush arrived in Washington with his faith-based initiatives, Paul W. Kingston observed that "undeniably, class theory has not had a prominent role in American sociology . . . This neglect is not surprising in the context of American culture . . . The very notion of class appears to contradict American ideals of equality and opportunity" (10). However, by the middle of the Bush era, literature such as the *New York Times'* acclaimed series of articles and the resultant book in 2005, *Class Matters*, demonstrated that these ideals of opportunity and equality in the United States had clearly become highly vulnerable and open to generalized debate.[6] Later, at the end of the Bush administration's mandate in 2008, Elizabeth Gudrais reported in *Harvard Magazine* that, "Income inequality has been rising since the late 1970s, and now rests at a level not seen since the Gilded Age—roughly 1870 to 1900, a period in U.S. history defined by the contrast between the excesses of the super-rich and the squalor of the poor" (23).

In general, as with the culture war, Bush was not at the origin of the negative conditions which characterized his administration. However, it is helpful to remember that Bush's faith-based program was nonetheless dispensed by an administration that presided over an extreme intensification of both economic and social stratification within the United States. Also, the above observations help to place the track record of the Bush administration within Lew Daly's description of the trends in American government leading up to 2006:

> [P]overty in the midst of plenty is the most basic moral reality any advanced nation must confront, but in the United States [it] is more than that. Here, poverty and plenty is a political way of life. And disturbingly, the apparent "desecularization" of recent decades (as some scholars are now calling it) seems only to have ingrained this contradiction more deeply: in no other country would shrinking the welfare rolls by more than half while millions fall into poverty be defined as a policy success . . . (*God and Welfare* xviii)

As Daly suggests, the intensity of the crisis in economic equality was mirrored, then, in the perceived or real abusiveness of the policies, faith-based included, being proffered as to how the growing social injustice could be curbed, contained, and addressed.

It can be argued that the intensification of economic and social stratification was a global event and that other advanced nations (for example in the European Union) were undergoing similar duress. And, indeed, few would deny that stratification stems from globalization as well as from an economy that increasingly benefits those with specific talents and positions (while penalizing others). Yet other nations were not specifically applying the same policy, nor seeking the same answers as the United States. In other words, faith-based policy could (or can) be seen, for example, as part of a devolution of sound government into a form of governance that, for a growing number of analysts,[7] is associated with an alleged rise in the power of interest groups.[8] Against the argument that governance represents enhanced participation in the democratic process (participatory governance), critics assert then, that governance is, in reality, a subterfuge for extending a system that threatens the public good.[9]

Further, if we keep in mind this backdrop of suspicion surrounding the notion of governance, it is helpful to underline Monsma and Soper's comment that as "governments look to private, often religiously-based organizations to play larger roles in society, questions of church and state are bound to be magnified" (2).[10] Although this may seem obvious, it is a necessary warning given that faith-based policy may certainly be seen as a part of a move from government to governance and that, logically, for many observers the question of interest groups and the respective responsibilities of church and state becomes all the more acute. Doubts arising from desecularisation, devolution, and increasing class-stratification created, therefore, a volatile environment in the "public square" of the Bush era for debate over the faith-based initiatives.

Given this context where the intricacies of church-state relations become acute, it was of the utmost importance that the policy be clearly represented to avoid confusion.[11] As Monsma and Soper implied, we may justifiably have a certain amount of trepidation concerning the application of a theory or vision in government policy when we know it has a religious origin. At the same time, we have seen in the case of principled pluralism, for example, that it demands toleration and posits religious and cultural pluralism as a foundation without which the vision loses its structural integrity. Perhaps this vision will or will not reassure us. Or, perhaps other characteristics inherent in principled pluralism will lead us to see these advocates of anti-interest group politics as, paradoxically, themselves an interest group. However, such clarity is needed to make an informed judgment about what is or is not at issue in a debate. We advance in chapters 5 and 6 that one of the major faults of the Bush administration on presenting social theory issuing from a religious perspective was a lack of precision about where its mission truly lay.

NOTES

1. This is a term used by José Casanova in *Public Religion in the Modern World* to describe a world-wide phenomenon in which "religion abandons its assigned place in the private sphere and enters the undifferentiated public sphere of civil society" (65).

2. For detail concerning the evolution of Charitable Choice into the Bush initiatives, see John Bartowski and Helen Regis' book, *Charitable Choices: Religion, Race, and Poverty in the Post-Welfare Era* (New York & London: New York University Press: 2003).

3. For a fuller description of key cases, see Stephen Monsma and Christopher Soper's *The Challenge of Pluralism: Church and State in Five Democracies*, 22–28.

4. *Everson v. Board of Education of Ewing Township*, 350 U.S. 15–16 (1947).

5. For a brief, but excellent historical survey of the Court's role in relation to religious questions, see Monsma and Soper's *The Challenge of Pluralism*, Chapter Two, "The United States: Strict Separation under Fire," 15–50.

6. A key element in the argument that the U.S. is classless is the inherent feature of upward social mobility in American society and in the above mentioned ideals of equality and opportunity. Yet as, Janny Scott and David Leonhardt observe in *Class Matters*, "new studies of mobility, which methodically track people's earnings over decades, have found far less movement. The economic advantage once believed to last only two or three generations is now believed to last closer to five . . . [One] study, by the Federal Bank of Boston, found that fewer families moved from one quintile, or of the income ladder to another during the 1980s than during the 1970s and that fewer moved in the 1990s than in the 1980s. A study by the Bureau of Labor Statistics also found that mobility declined from the 1980s to the 1990s" (21–22). In another study included in *Class Matters*, "The College Dropout Boom," Leonhardt also notes that "despite one of the great education explosions in modern history, economic mobility—moving from one income group to another over the course of a lifetime—has stopped rising . . . Some recent studies suggest that it has declined over the last generation" (90).

7. For more information concerning the concern felt over faith-based policies and the desecularisation or devolution of public, safety-net services to the private sector, see, for example: Gwendolyn Mink's "Faith in Government?" *Social Justice*, 28.1 (2001): 5–10; David Saperstein's "Public accountability and faith-based organizations: A problem best avoided." *Harvard Law Review*, 116.5 (2003): 1353–1396, and; Robert Wineburg's *Faith-based Inefficiency, the Follies of Bush's Initiatives* (Westport: CT: Praeger Publishers, 2007).

8. While governance is a term with an extremely wide variety of applications, its most classic use is to differentiate government (whether it be found in state or non-state, international, national, or local governing bodies) from the act(s) involved in governing. From this essentially administrative connotation, governance has, in much political, social, and government analysis, come to be associated with the exercise of political power.

9. For example, Sheldon Wolin offers a very concise and insightful analysis of the totalitarian threat to the public good and to popular sovereignty arising from what he terms "democracy incorporated." For more information see, *Democracy Incorporated; Managed Democracy and the Specter of Inverted Totalitarianism* (Princeton: Princeton University Press, 2008).

10. In their book, Monsma and Soper consider the question of pluralism not only in the United States, but in the context of a number of western countries.

11. And this is the case not only for those who are systematically against such policy, but for those who might have some sympathy or belief in its possible usefulness. In other words, clarity was necessary, not just in order to attain any hopes of success, but quite simply in order to provide Americans with their right to be able to form an honest appraisal of what it signified.

FIVE

From Theory to Application: Conflicting Signals

"Conflicting Signals" analyses the misunderstanding of the theology behind the faith-based policy during its introductory phase under the Bush
administration. Here principled pluralism and the religious right's ver-
sion(s) of it serve as reference points for: 1) illustrating and understanding the differing and often conflicting lines of thought that came to characterize the application of the faith-based initiative and; 2) clarifying the
danger in the extreme religious right's approach to the faith-based initiative.

The 2004 study, *Of Little Faith: The Politics of George W. Bush's Faith-
Based Initiatives*, provides an excellent illustration of the influence principled pluralism had in the thinking of the religious right. The authors
rightly underline the pivotal role of the Center for Public Justice in helping "politicians fashion legal arguments to support greater cooperation
between the government and religious providers of social services"
(Black, Koopman, and Ryden 48). Given this formative role, we may then
see how the policy of Bush could express this pluralist vision. First, as we
have seen, principled pluralists put ultimate value on associational life
because it creates and expresses what they consider to be the deepest
personal values and beliefs. This activity may therefore be considered
private or individual. Thus, programs such as the faith-based initiative
implicitly recognize the autonomy of voluntary organizations and associations in relation to the state. At the same time, the activity of associational life is also held by principled pluralists to be the most important civic
activity of those involved.[1] As a result, associational life is both public
and private. Acknowledging that associations and organizations must be
considered as intrinsically public, and not merely as private, the faith-
based initiative also responds to this facet of the pluralist vision.

In *Church, State and Public Justice: 5 Views*, principled pluralist Corwin Smidt succinctly provides four more explanations[2] delineating the relationship between principled pluralism and the faith-based initiative:

- such a policy "recognizes the structural pluralism evident within God's created order" (151). And this order recognizes both governmental and non-governmental efforts that work side by side to meet America's welfare needs.
- the faith-based initiative responds to the principled pluralist's view of neutrality within the framework of the Constitution rather than strict separation between church and state (151).
- the initiative recognizes the "confessional pluralism" which prevails in American society: "Neither atheists nor Christians, Jews nor Muslims, nor any other group can be excluded simply because of their particular religious beliefs" (151).
- The faith-based policy contained in Bush's initiative results from the acknowledgement, as we saw earlier, that "poverty has a moral and personal root that public funding is unable to address" (152).

For the thinkers who preceded and ultimately participated in the molding of the faith-based initiative, principled pluralism provided in the words of Carlson-Thies, the model and "language, which just wasn't available elsewhere" (Personal interview 26 Oct. 2012) for religious self-governance in social welfare.[3]

After the above considerations, it would seem, then, that the Bush Administration in 2001 was busily elaborating policy that would clearly express for all to see the principled pluralism of its architects. As John Dilulio observed when he assumed power in 2001, the faith-based initiative was being held up and forwarded as an expression of "Compassionate conservatism [which] warmly welcomes godly people back into the public square while respecting and upholding, without fail, our wise, benevolent constitutional traditions governing church, state, and civic pluralism" (Kemeny 12). The overriding and obvious reality is, however, that many perceived the policy as being anything but respectful of constitutional traditions and, in fact, extremely dangerous.

Certainly one reason for this fear is underlined by Dilulio himself in his later complaint that the initiative had from its introduction almost immediately become swamped in a "polarizing debate" (Personal interview). And notably, a very vocal camp in this agitation was made up of evangelical groups who, for example, were championing legalisation that would enable faith-based organizations to proselytise while receiving government funding (Leaming 19).[4] Nonetheless, beyond this evangelical call for proselytizing, which was ignored by the Bush administration, a much more fundamental and revealing explanation for the perceived dangers of the policy is perhaps indicated quite simply in Dilulio's message and his use of the term "compassionate conservatism." For as we will see in our analysis, the term may be said to be loaded with meanings and associations that, particularly filtered through the person of George W. Bush, illustrate the perceived, or real, dangers inherent in the policy. It is in this context, therefore, that we will see how a vision behind faith-based policy such as principled pluralism may be perceived as a far more reductive and threatening Protestant theory of social reform. Moreover, this exploration is useful not only for setting-off and clearly delineating theory, but also for clarifying perceptions of the policy that, perhaps inevitably, came to taint its subsequent reputation.

To illustrate the perceived dangers of the policy at the time of its introduction, our study turns to one of the most illustrious prophets of compassionate conservatism, Marvin Olasky and uses as a reference his 1992 best-seller, *The Tragedy of American Compassion*. Perhaps the member with the highest profile of what became known as the "purist"[5] faction (which includes the likes of Charles Murray and George Grant),[6] Olasky wanted faith-based legislation that resisted any compromise over the faith-based organizations' total freedom to run government-funded programs as they saw fit. In other words, he was part of the vocal camp fighting for the above-mentioned right to proselytize. What is arguably more important, though, is that he was doing it: 1) in the name of compassionate conservatism and; 2) in the name of being the movement's "godfather."[7] It is true that there are no polls or scientific studies establishing exactly how much Olasky and his brand of conservative compassion defined faith-based policy in the minds of potential, and logically, partisan antagonists who were either unfamiliar with, or vague about, the theory behind it. However, as we will see, it is fair to say that it is a brand that provides a framework within which the policy could not help but be perceived.

Through his book, Olasky was held up by many as being the authority in the 1990s on the question of compassion and giving. Consider, for example: 1) the references used in former Republican Speaker Newt Gingrich's first address to the nation: "Our models are Alexis de Tocqueville and Marvin Olasky. We are going to redefine compassion and take it back" (Grann 64); 2) Gingrich's insistence when, as Speaker, he made Olasky's *The Tragedy of American Compassion* required reading for freshman Republican members of Congress; 3) the extensive literature that, in general, attests to Olasky's undeniably central role in the expansion of the American focus "beyond the growth of government welfare" (Donaldson and Carlson-Thies 37) and; 4) the ramifications stemming from the fervent admiration of then-Governor George W. Bush. Indeed, Olasky's type of "compassionate conservatism" was integral in the formation of Bush's perceptions concerning the possible role religious organizations could or should play in providing social aid and in his mid-90s defense of the faith-based substance abuse program, Teen Challenge. It can also be seen in the 1996 Governor's Advisory Task Force on Faith-Based Community Service Groups, where Olasky teamed with the more moderate Carlson-Thies, and legal expert, Carl Exbeck (like Carlson-Thies, Esbeck later worked with the Bush administration), to elaborate the resultant report, *Faith in Action: A New Vision for Church—State Cooperation in Texas.* A final illustration of the influence of the Olaskian vision on Bush is found in the president's well-known "Forward" to Olasky's *Compassionate Conservatism: What It Is, What It Does, and How It Can Transform America.*[8]

It is true that when Bush became president, he had already begun to distance himself from Olasky's radical, evangelical vision, with the result that Olasky had very little to do with the actual elaboration of the administration's policy. This task was delegated to the likes of Carlson-Thies. Moreover, Olasky progressively distanced himself as time passed from a policy he felt was far too moderate (Carlson-Thies Personal interview 3). Nevertheless, it is revealing that when one of Bush's aides was asked before the election what a compassionate conservative administration might look like, the reply was simply, "Talk to Marvin" (Grann 64). Given the blurring of boundaries between the public president and the private evangelical that typified Bush even before his presidency,[9] Olasky's vision: 1) helps us to elucidate (at the very least) both the roots and the characteristics of the perceived threat that accompanied the advent of Bush's faith-based policy and; 2) serves as a powerful illustration of the way(s) in which faith-based policy could be perceived as something more extreme and threatening than anything forwarded by principled pluralists (like Carlson-Thies), or Catholics (like Dilulio).

With these objectives in mind, we can first note that in *The Tragedy of American Compassion*, Olasky methodically applies what may be construed as being certain aspects of principled pluralism to early colonial American history. And as Daly notes, Olasky shares Christian Democratic influences with principled pluralists such as those found in the Center for Public Justice.[10] Nonetheless, in so doing, he not only transforms the spirit of principled pluralism, but engenders a religiously extreme vision of American history and identity.

More specifically, a brief survey of the fundamental values that together make up Olasky's early American model for compassion demonstrates that they reflect loosely the associational spheres of influence inherent in principled pluralism. At the same time, Olasky's version of the model comes in the semblance of a systematic study in which all of his assertions concerning the early American values behind compassionate giving are based on historical fact.[11] In fact, Olasky sees the colonial period as a virtuous past in which, as David Hammack notes, the "American people followed godly and (hence) effective social care practices based in revealed religion (259).[12] Hammack then details these practices as including the direct, personal provision of spiritual and material care by relatives wherever possible, [13] by neighbors, [14] or by the local church; hospitality to victims of disaster; the provision of poorhouses and charity schools [15] for all poor children; a sometimes confrontational insistence on decent living by recipients of help; and a willingness to withhold assistance from those who were not worthy. (259) [16]

Keeping in mind Hammack's observation that the compassionate person provides not only "material," but also "spiritual" (259) care, we can see how Olasky moves on to the contention that "the most important need of the poor who were unfaithful was to learn about God and God's expectations for man" (8–9). In other words, in the Olaskian worldview, compassion and Christianity are inextricably associated.

The primary and essential problem to be already underlined in Olasky's vision is that its assertions are not in fact based on a true account of early American history. Olasky seems to select what he wishes to see, with the result that much of his argument quite simply disintegrates on close examination. For example, the reader is provided with the misleading impression that the colonial period can be characterized as being homogenous and static. As most students of early American history know, the colonies were certainly not homogeneous and applying a model of common values to Puritans, Quakers, Anglicans, and Catholics is a perilous venture. Similarly, forms of social aid during the period between Jamestown and the American Revolution were not static. [17] In short, the homogenous, anti-pluralist, Calvinist national identity portrayed as a model is an illusion.

As his book moves forward in time, one of Olasky's most extraordinary reinterpretations of nineteenth-century history is based on his neglect to even acknowledge the bitter division and quarrelling between various Protestant groups or the prejudice against Catholics. Going beyond denominational boundaries in his book, Olasky is obviously intent on showing the spiritual vantage point of what he feels is necessary to be efficiently compassionate. But through his selectiveness, it also seems that he is intent on referencing and recreating a sort of Calvinist "Jerusalem on the hill." As Carlson-Thies demonstrates in the following quote, this vision is very much at odds with the principled pluralist and subsidiarity worldview of religion in society:

[T]he proponents of principled pluralism/sphere sovereignty (perhaps in distinction from some others who favored and pushed for the Bush faith-based initiative) did not see the goal as being some reassertion of official Christian public influence, but rather the removal of public policies and attitudes that wrongly were biased against a fair opportunity for religious organizations and ideas to be present in public life and in partnership with government. That is, the appeal was to a "level playing field," with an open competition of ideas and values, and not to a return to some presumed previous predominance. ("Comments")

If Olasky shares such a position, it remains that he certainly doesn't give the impression in what amounts to a reinterpretation of American history. It also remains that if one is so preoccupied with demonstrating what are held to be universal values for a nation, the exclusivist nature of their reality in practice cannot be ignored.

A very short selection of illustrations helps us to see that this reductive vision of what made America work is extended in Olasky's treatment of subsequent American history.[18] Of particular interest is Olasky's dismissive portrayal of national foundations and organizations that were collectively attempting to improve American welfare throughout the first half of the twentieth century.[19] This goes against the principled pluralist and subsidiarity view of what makes up a diversified, pluralistic society in relation to the distribution of social services. Such organizations play a vital role in the overall integrity of a healthy polity and are not simply to be ignored. Neither is there mention of the role government played in progressively developing independence in Americans (and not dependence) through the creation of educational opportunities, both in the form of public schooling or in such efforts as the GI Bill for World War II veterans.

However, the worst for Olasky was not to come until the 1960s. Before the Great Society, he writes, "recipients themselves often viewed welfare as a necessary wrong, but not a right. Two gatekeepers—the welfare office and the applicant's own conscience—scrutinized each applicant . . . [There was] a sense of shame" (167). The Great Society is to be condemned first of all for advocating a war on this sense of shame (168) and secondly for advancing the mistaken "cash was king" (171) belief that federal spending could eliminate poverty in America. By 1980, the results of the Great Society had, according to Olasky, brought about a decline in: social mobility; in private aid organizations; in individual giving; and finally in the institution of marriage (190).

Olasky does not balance these observations with any discussion at all of the virtual elimination of abject poverty among America's elderly achieved through Medicare, Medicaid, and the expansion of social security. Nor does he breathe a word about ambitious projects like Head Start, college student loan programs, or the other multitude of forms that federal aid took in education. And, strikingly, he ignores completely the civil rights movement.[20] Here, in one context, principled pluralists such as Skillen, Mouw or Carlson-Thies are in agreement with Olasky. They feel (as we have seen) that the naïve (or false liberal, Enlightenment) belief in the all-encompassing power of the state to "do it all," as Lyndon Johnson proclaimed in the optimism of the period, translated into interest group politics. Johnson's War on Poverty thus ultimately proved to be a noble, but inefficient means of rectifying injustices in society. At the same time, in my interviews with Mouw (Personal interview 22 Feb. 2010) and Carlson-Thies (Personal interview 19 Feb. 2010), neither of them denied the positive effects that such programs did have on the United States. While they are certainly not liberals, they are not extremists like Olasky.

Mouw and Carlson-Thies are working more in the context of the neo-conservative, who is, by definition, attempting to find answers in the backwash of Great Society failures. Consider, then, the far more balanced analysis of the performance by the Great Society in *A Revolution of Compassion* (37–39) where, even when the principled pluralists find fault in the secularized Great Society experiment, the description concentrates not so much on the faults of the program, but rather on the paradox arising from the faith-based identity of so many of the program's social aid providers. In other words, for principled pluralists like Mouw and Carlson-Thies, the attempt to establish efficient delivery in social services is based on an assessment that is less rigid, less dogmatic, and less dismissive than Olasky's.

In general, we see that Olasky's selective and reductive vision of what has worked in America conflicts with principled pluralism's assertion that the different spheres (whether they be faith-based or secular) are both useful and necessary in creating a healthy polity. However, we can note that it is true that Olasky's vision does affirm the vital role of communities and associations. Also, like principled pluralists, Olasky admittedly does see society in the context of some sort of cultural self-governance. And finally, his vision, like the one of the principled pluralist is based on a teleological process where God is revealed in history. Nonetheless, it remains that he is totally at odds with principled pluralism's ideal of an organic order where the autonomy of the parts is meant to ensure the order of the whole, where government can and does have a role and where there can be no favoritism concerning a faith or a nonfaith. In short, after affirming the positive effects of, for example, Medicare, foundations, or government educational programs, principled pluralist Carlson-Thies affirmed that Olasky was a catalyst in creating the conversation which led to the faith-based initiatives, but that in a sort of logical circle, he was that catalyst because he was without a doubt a "firebrand" (Personal interview 19 Feb. 2010).

Make no mistake, both principled pluralism and the vision advocated by Olasky are both forms of social aid which would have been unthinkable in the not-too-distant past. Nonetheless, through the selective and reductive method used to depict it, Olasky's picture of America may easily be perceived as contradicting the key concept which defines any possibility of success and approbation for faith-based policy, moderation. David Gergen illustrates this belief in moderation, while also delineating against the backdrop of Olsaky's model, both the similarities and differences inherent in a more responsible approach to the role of faith:

> There is nothing to fear from an infusion of people of faith into our politics; indeed, they should be welcomed. After all, people of strong

faith helped to create some of our noblest causes, including the aboli-
tionist movement in the nineteenth century and the civil rights movement of the twentieth. Just because many of today's most ardent
churchgoers come from the right is no excuse for people on the left to
now say that religion must be kept out of politics. A people's values are
inevitably rooted in its spiritual beliefs. But we do have reason to say a
firm aggressive "No" to extremists on either side who try to impose
their religious—or secular—beliefs upon the rest of us. (58)

Given Olasky's selective method, then the best we can say is that, in some
cases, he considers only certain aspects of what has worked. The worst
we can say is that his generalizations on compassion are ungrounded and
so extreme that he is unable to acknowledge any viable contribution
made by other contradictory models.

A first question is how such a vision of a mythologized past like
Olasky's could gain so much influence with a faction of the religious
right.[21] A good indication of the answer is found in Newt Gingrich's
statement that Olasky "goes back 300 years and looks at what has worked
in America . . ." (75). As we have seen, the explanation for what "works"
in Olasky's vision cannot be found in good historical research. Rather, as
David Hammock notes, the only way Olasky's method can be said to
work is if it has as its basis the "centrality of revealed religion [and] the
innate sinfulness of mankind" (Hammock 264). *The Tragedy of American
Compassion* is in fact, then, a jeremiad. Richard E. Wentz explains that

Whenever the towns and colonies of New England faced a crisis . . .
people were reminded that . . . some form of disobedience, a breaking
of the covenant was at the root of the crisis . . . [T]he jeremiad consisted
of a description of the crisis, a reminder of the covenant, a renewal of
obedience and [warnings] should there be insufficient renewal of the
covenant. (197–98)

And *The Tragedy of American Compassion* blames current troubles "on a
moral corruption [resulting from government] that has produced a fall
from a projected society lost in a golden past" (Hammock).[22] While un-
scientific by the traditional standards of the historian, Olasky's method
generally makes perfect sense, therefore, in a teleological vision con-
toured by extremely conservative evangelical thought. Given this context, we see why a certain faction of the religious right would never
accuse Olasky of being reductive. On the contrary, supporters of Olasky
can assert that even if he is selective, he "got his history right" by correctly emphasizing what God has revealed in American history.

A second question concerns the danger that may be seen in such a
vision as Olasky's. One obvious perceived danger is found in the flip side
of what Olasky's supporters appreciate in his version of history, the "centrality of revealed religion." In other words, the same vision has often
sustained the critique[23] as tending towards, if not expressing, Dominion-

ism, or more specifically, "Reformed Dominionism."[24] Note that it is not a question here of whether Olasky can be defended in some way against such a charge (Olasky considers himself a "Christian libertarian").[25] Neither is it a question of whether such a heavy judgment may be argued by some as revealing the shock of certain commentators on seeing a version of history that assigns such a central and public role to religion. The point here is, quite simply, that the selective method used in Olasky's version of American history lends itself to this perception, even amongst moderate commentators of faith-based policy.[26]

A further danger is related to the unprecedented centrality of "values politics" since the Reagan era and that there has been a trend in American politics, political discourse and mass marketing in which providing factual truth about values is second to finding a responsive chord in the population (White 4–6).[27] As has also been clear since Reagan, many Americans: 1) do feel a strong affinity for values such as individualism, self-reliance, and a strong family, and; 2) do identify such values as traditionally American. An Olaskyian view of compassion plays to this profound sentiment while blithely neglecting the numerous achievements that associational, foundational, or governmental effort has provided. As a result, many of the values promoted by the vision undoubtedly "ring true" for the majority of Americans. Yet, the method behind the selection of facts deforms the mirror that Olasky is holding up. In short, between the American affinity for traditional values and this misleading presentation of American identity, *The Tragedy of American Compassion* lays threatening groundwork for the possible manipulation of the American people's self-perception.

Finally, our last question concerns the role Olasky's vision played in the perception of what was behind the Bush faith-based initiative. As we mentioned, there is no concrete measure of the degree to which Olasky's brand of "compassionate conservatism" framed, or still frames, the perception of faith-based policy for those unversed in the actual theory behind it. On the other hand, much of the terror critics felt and wrote about when faced with Bush's faith-based policy was based on perceptions which situated it far more in the Olaskian universe than that of principled pluralism and subsidiarity. Also, it is undeniable that Olaskian compassionate conservatism served as ammunition for partisan antagonists. Perhaps most interestingly, though, supporters of the policy bear witness to the reality of Olasky's shadow (and his mythologized vision of America) through their preoccupation with the perception of the policy. And this preoccupation is even tacitly acknowledged in the terminology used in their arguments. Consider Carlson-Thies and Donaldson's method of presenting the policy in *A Revolution of Compassion*, where they use the categories "myth" as opposed to "reality" when defending the tenets and principles behind the policy against the stereotypes that characterize them. DiIulio uses the same technique in *Godly Republic*. What is generally clear, then, is that Olasky's nationalistic, ultra-conservative vision undoubtedly sent out, in a variety of ways, conflicting signals about what the Bush faith-based policy meant. And in so doing, it was a burden to an administration which was attempting to assert its viability in relation to the pluralism "promised in the Constitution."

NOTES

1. Associational life is political in nature since it seeks "to address issues of the polis broadly conceived and to engage the broad interests and concerns of citizens" (Thiemann 132).

2. For a concise, detailed description of principled pluralism and public policy, see Smith, 150–53.

3. This explanation is mirrored by other preeminent legal specialists and leaders of the religious right. For example, Jay Sekulow of the influential American Center for Law and Justice "follows a cultural-mandate approach, as set out in Kuyper's best-known proclamation of world-view theology . . . " (Daly *God and Welfare* 64).

4. We will come back to the story of DiIulio and the administration's positioning in this introductory phase of the policy in chapter 6.

5. For more information, see *Of Little Faith*, 115–17.

6. For a brief, but concise description of these personalities, see Davy's *God and the Welfare State*, 69–72.

7. Olasky was widely regarded as "the godfather of [the] compassionate conservatism" (Grann 62) behind the 1996 Welfare Act and the faith-based initiative.

8. See Olasky's *Compassionate Conservatism: What It Is, What It Does, and How It Can Transform America* (New York: The Free Press, 2000) xi–xiii.

9. We will come back more fully to the persona of Bush and the identification of his administration as a right-wing, evangelical juggernaut in the next chapter.

10. See Daly's *God and the Welfare State*, 71–72.

11. Olasky grounds his model on what he considers to be three defining characteristics of colonial life: 1) Olasky cites Pilgrim leader William Bradford's description of how his group faced illness and want, as a reference for the voluntary spirit necessary in giving (6); 2) Olasky then gives documentation from the minutes of the Fairfield Connecticut town council meeting of April 16, 1673, in order to support his contention that the early American model for compassion also emphasized "hospitality" (7) and 3); Olasky cites groups such as the Scots' Charitable Society as proof of his assertion that those in need must merit help. Olasky states that "the open hand was not extended to all" (7).

12. Olasky's belief that God was not "merely the establisher of principles but a personal intervener" (8) leads to the first and most basic of four theological themes which further determine (after the above mentioned characteristics) his early American model of compassion: In short, as an image of God, man must go beyond what Olasky calls "clockwork charity" and give truly out of love (8).

13. Olasky contends that "Nothing that could contribute to the breakup of families or to the lessening of the family's central role as support of its members was encouraged" (13).

14. In this process of neighbourly care, Olasky highlights the importance of personal interaction between provider and recipient. Olasky, however, does not see the primary importance of personal contact with the needy as a prerequisite for giving as part of a loving, I-thou, compassionate relationship. Rather, personal knowledge of the "distinct character" of each needy person was (is) necessary for ultimately deciding whether or not they were deserving of aid (8).

15. Olasky illustrates different colonial applications of Elizabethan Poor Law in order to reinforce his version of early compassion. For example, the institution of work

houses and charity schools for poor children is used to prove the effectiveness and applicability of the early American model of compassion.

16. Olasky both develops and documents the theme of "withholding charity at times" (9) far more than the others. Olasky consequently affirms that "Today's believers in 'liberation theology' often argue that God is on the side of the poor, but the older distinction (the early America model) showed God backing the mistreated poor and chastising those who had indulged in indolence" (8).

17. For example, political and economic forces in the early 1700s began "to erode the authority of the family, church, and government throughout the colonies" (Hall 17) with a resultant, inverse growth in voluntary organizations. Furthermore, Olasky's descriptions of early American life stress the independence of the church from the government, and the seemingly natural cohesion between church and community. In reality, many colonies had tax-supported churches which a large number of colonists considered oppressive (Butler 188). Likewise, Olasky's illustrations, which suggest the uniform application of the Elizabethan Poor Law, are misleading. As Peter Hall notes, "The adoption of English law and legal forms did not begin in any significant way before the 1790's. And even then, it occurred in a selective fashion, framed by local and regional concerns" (16).

18. For example, eager to create and substantiate the myth of an Early American Model of Compassion based on religious commitment, he says nothing about the conflicts that led first to the disestablishment of religion in Virginia, and then to the entire nation (through the First Amendment, and subsequent comparable provisions in the state constitutions).

19. A concise illustration of the productive efforts and results obtained by foundations, associations and organizations is found in Ruth Hutchinson Crocker's *Social Work and Social Order: the Settlement Movement of Two Industrial Cities, 1889–1930* (Champaign: University of Illinois Press, 1992) 1–9. A more complete analysis of these results is provided by *States, Social Knowledge and the Origins of Modern Social Policies*. Eds. Dietrich Rueschemeyer and Theda Skocpal. (Princeton: Princeton University Press and New York: Russel Sage Foundation, 1996).

20. Olasky's omission reveals the conservative perspective that Great Society programs did not come from the civil rights movement, but from a generally white, "elite" self-serving intelligentsia. A perspective which argues that this "new class self-interest was particularly evident, according to the conservative critics, in the liberal social welfare agenda. Though social programs might have been designed to help the poor, they actually enriched and empowered the 'social engineers' who designed them and the army of bureaucrats and professionals who staffed them. Reflecting the mainstream right-wing view, the *National Review* editorialized that the poor themselves had very little to do with social welfare policy, other than to serve as pawns of new-class strategists" (Ehrenreich 168).

21. There are a number of analyses which are useful for suggesting why there is the necessity for a mythologized past. Barbara Ehrenreich's study, "The New Right Attack on Social Welfare," is notably excellent for general discussion of the socio-economic necessities which lead to such a stance.

22. Unlike the best of his seventeenth-century predecessors, however, Olasky emphasizes the discourse of those who misled the American public more than he does the sins and delusions of the public itself.

23. See, for example, Michelle Goldberg's *Kingdom Coming: The Rise of Christian Nationalism* (Rotterdam: Sense Publishers, 2011) 51–52.

24. Reformed Dominionism is called so because of its roots in the neo-Calvinist thought of the Reformed Church. Also called Christian Reconstructionism, it forwards the belief that God is the sole authority in a society governed by biblical law. This view of society and public ethics is called "theonomy." In its contemporary form, Christian Reconstructionism began with Rousas John Rushdoony and was carried forward in the latter part of the twentieth century with followers such as Jerry Falwell, Pat Robertson, D. James Kennedy, and Francis Shaefler. We might also note that there are

other forms of Dominionism such as the more charismatic, Pentecostal movement created in the 1980s, and based on what is called "Kingdom Now Theology." A relative new-comer is the New Apostolic Reformation, which dates from 1996 and was founded by C. Peter Wagner. This movement is unique in that it forwards a non-democratic infrastructure run by a hierarchy of new "Apostles."

25. Perhaps not surprisingly, "Olasky does not think his religious extremism is radical" (Goldberg 52).

26. For example, Daly, who presents a very balanced and objective view of faith-based policy, describes Olasky in the same breath as George Grant (*God and Welfare* 71–72). And Grant, as Daly observes, "envisioned an army of churches arising from the ashes of welfare reform and establishing a beachhead for wider Christian dominion. He believed that public programs should be dismantled and religious charity renewed" (*God and Welfare* 69).

27. What counts is that the values expressed "ring true" with the population.

SIX

Theory in Application: Conflicting Use of the Instruments

Resolutely focusing his campaign on domestic policy, George W. Bush was equally adamant about not wanting to become a "nation builder" or a president unduly subject to the distractions of foreign policy. In *God's Economy: Faith-Based Initiatives and the Caring State*, Lew Daly underscores the paradoxical fate reserved for the "domestic" president:

> That his presidency will be remembered for little else reflects the extraordinary impact of September 11 on American foreign policy and political institutions, but also on American religious debates. Bush's crusade in the Muslim world sparked for many, a simplistic, dangerous vision of clashing civilizations and global conflict between good and evil. But an important secondary effect, no less devastating, was its crowding out of the religious debate he was actually prepared to have when he came to Washington. (3)

A central pawn in this general debate was, of course, the Faith-Based and Community Initiative. And, as Daly observes, its effort at leveling the playing field would ultimately be conditioned by the devastating aftereffects of 9/11. More specifically, though, while Daly's take on the general situation is exact, we must be perfectly clear that 9/11 did not have the easily identifiable impact on faith-based policy that may be so spectacularly seen in the context of foreign policy, homeland security, or even airport safety. In the case of the initiatives it is rather in the timing of the event and its relation to the developments within the Bush administration and Congress.

We will study how these developments worked in concert to create substantial, and arguably catastrophic, collateral damage to the effectiveness of the policy. To illustrate how 9/11 had an influence on the develop-

49

ment and execution of the FBCI, I will first provide a necessary, but brief description of the program leading up to the event. Here we will review: 1) the characteristics of the relatively solid consensus concerning faith-based policy that was demonstrated in the political debate during the 2000 presidential election; and 2) the Bush administration's confused and confusing performance to enact, despite this consensus, the initiative before 9/11. Having this background, we will then evaluate how 9/11 had a subsequent impact on faith-based policy and its performance. I will highlight in my analysis the trajectory of the Director of the White House Office of Faith-Based and Community Initiatives (OFBCI) at the time of the attacks, John Dilulio Jr. As mentioned in the introduction, Dilulio serves not only as an efficient vehicle for depicting the events leading up to 9/11 and the fall-out it had on the faith-based effort, but also as a filter for our conclusions concerning both the Bush administration's faith-based effort as well as key characteristics of American support.

In the early days of the 2000 presidential election, one of the candidates stated that the American people's "severest challenges are not just material, but spiritual." The candidate expanded on the theme, declaring that:

> For too long, national leaders have been trapped in a dead-end debate. Some on the right have said for too long that a specific set of religious values should be imposed, threatening the founders' precious separation of church and state. In contrast, some on the left have said for too long that religious values should play no role in addressing public needs. . . . [F]reedom of religion need not mean freedom from religion . . . There is a better way. . . . Ordinary Americans have decided to confront the fact that our severest challenges are not just material, but spiritual . . . [F]aith- and values-based organizations show a strength that goes beyond "volunteerism." These groups nationwide have shown a muscular commitment to facing down poverty, drug addictions, domestic violence and homelessness. And when they have worked out a partnership with government, they have created programs and organizations that have woven a resilient web of life support under the most helpless among us. . . . Today I give you this pledge; if you elect me President, the voice of faith-based organizations will be integral to the policies set forth in my administration. (Gore)

Though one can almost picture George W. Bush eyeing the audience and mouthing the above words, the speaker is in fact the Democratic presidential candidate, Al Gore. Made while campaigning at the Salvation Army Center in Atlanta, Georgia, the speech corroborates Dilulio's observation that in what was often a contentious presidential campaign, one consistent consensus point for both candidates was their wish to create an "even playing field," regulated by "faith-friendly national laws" (*Godly* 84).

After the 1996–2000 charitable choice laws signed during the Clinton administration, this sentiment of consensus cannot be considered, as we have already seen, to necessarily be something radically new. However, the 2000 election was an important signpost indicating that such policy had (perhaps quietly) been acquiring increasingly wide support within the Democratic Party, and that this trend would continue. Consider, for example, Hillary Clinton's position in January, 2005:

> who is more likely to go out onto a street to save some poor, at-risk child than . . . someone who believes in the divinity of every person, who sees God at work in the lives of even the most hopeless and left-behind of our children? And that's why we need to not have a false division or debate about the role of faith-based institutions; we need to just do it and provide the support that is needed on an ongoing basis" (qtd, in Dilulio and Kuo).

This continued bi-partisan support for a faith-based policy reinforces the assertion by faith-based pioneers like Carlson-Thies and Dilulio that, in reality, faith-based policy has been the product of a consensual, non-partisan, long-term process, beginning in the Clinton administration, and subsequently supported by presidential candidates Al Gore and George W. Bush in 2000, John Kerry and Bush in 2004, and both Hillary Clinton and Barack Obama in 2008. Specifically considered within the context of the impending Bush presidency, the salient fact to call attention to is that support of faith-based programs and charitable choice laws in 1999 and 2000 was not the exclusive domain of the right-wing. On the contrary, it was a policy which appealed to a relatively broad political spectrum.

That the Bush administration was not able to apply such policy may be explained by an antagonism between Democrat and Republican that set in almost immediately after Bush took power. Tracing this antago-nism back to the controversial circumstances which surrounded Bush's election, Dilulio, for example, maintains that fall-out from the vote-count controversy[1] in the 2000 election politically handicapped the pre-9/11 Bush White House "to a degree that has yet to be duly appreciated, even by careful observers" (Personal interview). The specific effects concern-ing Bush's faith-based policy is captured in the following observation:

> Bush had sought the office as a centrist "compassionate conservative" who had distanced himself explicitly from the "destructive" idea that merely cutting government was next to godliness. Upon entering office in January 2001, he faced a no-honeymoon Congress. Many Democrats, even centrists, were in full partisan attack mode. Congressional Repub-licans and their conservative loyalists were ready to rally to the new president's defense. They did, but at a price. (*Godly* 113)

Republican religious extremists were thus not the only ones, as some analysts have asserted, who undermined the possibility of success for

faith-based policy under Bush.[2] Equally being a predetermined objective
of the Democrats, this effort at crippling the policy was truly bipartisan.

In a climate where the Democrats were not about to give Bush any
kind of grace period, it quickly became the general sentiment that nothing was going to come easily, or at all, for the Bush faith-based effort (all
of the actors behind the policy I interviewed concurred on this appraisal).
In this light, Dilulio specifically remembers a conversation in February
2001 with an apologetic Democratic Congressional leader who confided
that "there is no desire to let the president get credit or win big through
compromise [and that] the charitable choice consensus would remain
buried for some time to come . . . Whatever the president says about
[faith-based programs], the focus through 2004 will be on what the people on his right [in the House] and other extremists say about them (*Godly*
114). However, it is also true that political use of religious issues reciprocally constituted a major offensive weapon to be deployed against Democrats by Republican strategists (even moderates).

According to the Republican strategy, such issues would serve not
only to keep Democrats off balance and defensive, but also to ultimately
polarize them as being secular and anti-religious. In an exchange with
one such strategist, Dilulio observes with despair that "Far from capital-
izing on bipartisan church-state sentiments and mass support, faith-
based initiatives, the strategist summarized, should contain proposals
that 'force Democrats' into opposition and make it easier to depict Democrats in Congress, even the faith-friendly centrists among them, as America's 'anti-God squad'" (*Godly* 113–114). This translates into the prerequisite where Republican support for Bush's No Child Left Behind education bill was tendered only with the understanding that it would be the
unique cooperative effort they would assent to make in applying such
policy. This limited gesture of support evidenced in No Child essentially
delineated the limits to which Republicans were willing to go in supporting any meaningful compassion issue slated on Bush's bi-partisan agenda (Dilulio Personal interview).

An added feature of the growing antagonism between Democrat and
Republican is found in Dilulio's above-assertion that conservative loyal-
ists rallied to Bush "at a price." In other words, more extreme members of
the religious-right, who were in reality highly critical (or opposed) to the
centrist message of the original Bush faith-based plan, refrained from
criticism during the presidential campaign and essentially toed the line.
Describing this faction of Bush supporters, both Michael Gerson (Personal interview) and Dilulio (Personal Interview) explained how Bush's
"Duty of Hope" speech drew intensely negative reactions from the Party's right wings, whether they were "tax-hating libertarians" or "Bible
beating extremists." Dilulio, who worked on the speech, added that it
went through more that sixteen pain-staking rewrites. Nonetheless, he
observed that, "numerous Republican conservative activists hated the

center-hugging compassionate conservatism" (Personal interview). The result is that once elected, Bush and his bi-partisan, moderate approach quickly fell prey to the extremists who went public with their opposition. The Bush administration was consequently subject to pressures, first of all, to take on the Court's neutrality, or equal protection doctrine. As we have seen, this doctrine was a key reason behind the already mentioned enabling role that the court system played in laying the groundwork for the progressive deprivatisation of religion and the consequent possibility of Bush's policy.

Jeopardizing this key tool for desecularization, Bush was called on by extremists to alter existing charitable choice laws, as well as to create new laws so that federal funding could be utilized for proselytizing (Dilulio Personal interview). While not supportive of the above-mentioned objectives, more moderate members of the Christian right also joined in with extremists in a further demand for co-religionist hiring policies. Note that the qualification "more moderate" is used to distinguish these Christians not only because they were against objectives such as proselytizing, but also because they did not feel that their position necessitated any transformation of existing law. Proponents of co-religionist hiring based (and base) their position on the following interpretation of the 1964 Civil Rights Act:

> For forty years, [The Act] has respected the right of religious groups to make religiously based employment decisions. Title VII of this Act— which is supported by Republicans and Democrats alike—protects Americans from employment discrimination based on race, color, religion, sex, and national origin. It also protects the ability of faith-based organizations to maintain their religious liberty and identity by hiring employees who share their religious beliefs. ("Protecting the Civil Rights" 1)

Because of the legal grounding of this particular issue,[3] it will be from the outset the greatest single source of continuing debate raised by the application of faith-based policy.

Specifically in the context of the pre-9/11 Faith-Based Office, the already growing conflict between supporter and foe of the co-religionist position, combined with the controversy generated by the other more extremist demands, serve to spotlight the daunting task faced by Dilulio and his staff in their initial struggle to develop some kind of coherent plan for application of the policy, And it is not surprising, then, that Dilulio very soon upon his arrival found himself in a "messy battle with Republican staff from the House of Representatives" (Personal interview).

In an effort to sabotage the original White House plan being promoted by Dilulio and his team, Republicans also distributed diverse versions of potential Bush faith bills which contained direct challenges to the constitutional neutrality principles embodied by charitable choice laws.[4] This problem of disinformation was compounded by "leaks" shared with the Washington media of supposed covert White House dealings with faith-based organizations. One of the most sensational examples was the front-page story published by the *Washington Post* on July 10, 2001, that asserted a secret White House deal exempting the Salvation Army from state and local employment antidiscrimination laws through a federal waiver. However, as Dilulio recounts, "it soon became clear to everyone that the information within this document was false and that there had never been any kind of deal and that no such deal had ever even been contemplated" (*Godly* 134). Carslon-Thies corroborates this, noting that he had participated in all the meetings with the Salvation Army "and there was no deal proposed" ("Comment"). Faced with so much subterfuge, it was in large part through the titanic effort and resistance of Dilulio that his concerns about the House bill's controversial provisions finally, albeit briefly, became in June 2001, the official position forwarded by the White House. All the same, after a battle that Dilulio qualified as surreal, the final draft of the Community Solutions Act of 2001 presented numerous problems for charitable-choice-friendly Democrats and Republicans, including Dilulio.[5]

First of all, despite efforts by Dilulio and certain members of Congress for bipartisanship, the bill (also known as H.R. 7) eventually passed by the House in July was acknowledged as having been a partisan effort (though, as already mentioned, it represented the only major faith-based legislation championed by the Republicans in Congress). Secondly (and logically), it was couched in troubling language clearly favoring the conservative-"purist" religious camp. As Daly observes:

> HR 7's charitable choice provisions were more aggressive than existing law in several sensitive areas. It introduced more specific language permitting federal preemption of state anti-discrimination laws under charitable choice, and it weakened beneficiary protections against proselytization. Another change introduced later, of critical interest to religious conservatives, was a provision permitting the executive branch to "voucherize" grant programs[6] without congressional approval, thereby removing constitutional barriers to government funding of otherwise prohibited religious activities and content . . . (*God's Economy* 61)[7]

The bill thus became portrayed as "a sop to the religious right." Moreover, faced with the obstacle of a Senate dominated by an antagonistic Democratic majority, it became increasingly apparent that there was little chance for any expansion of charitable choice through an act of legislation. Such were the partisan forces as they were arrayed in the summer of 2001.

Faced with such a volatile political landscape, prospects in general for the Bush administration's faith-based policy seemed, at best, bleak. The return of Congress to business as usual in September 2001 clearly represented a critical period in the life of the initiative within the legislative process. Moreover, Carslon-Thies, Dilulio, and presidential advisor Michael Gerson all agreed that any remaining chance for legislation would have demanded a world-moving ("perhaps miraculous," in Dilulio's words) effort.

What 9/11 first represented in relation to this faith-based effort was a world-moving event that, given the American population's reaction, resulted in an environment that was arguably conducive to a successful legislative effort. For example, Black, Koopman, and Ryden observe that "in the wake of September 11, church attendance and attack-related charitable activities by churches increased; there was, in the American public, an extended rise in pro-religious behavior and attitudes" (166). They also add that "For the two weeks surrounding Thanksgiving Day 2001, the possibility of a bill from the Senate by the end of the year seemed quite good" (167).[8] In short, a successful campaign for the initiative was theoretically possible. However, given the divisive political environment, such a campaign would have taken all the careful attention, precise explanation, and administrative flair that the Bush team could summon. This did not happen: the second and most obvious result of 9/11 was to distract the president's and his administration's attention away from these critical challenges (Gerson Personal interview). Also, based on his experience in the White House, Gerson adds that only a small reduction in an American president's attention time can have relatively dramatic policy results (Personal interview). Dilulio summarizes the effects of the terrorist attacks in his observation that "the post-9/11 reality changed things for the Bush presidency, including putting domestic and social policy on hold for months" (Afterword 298). Victim of this new orientation, the faith-based issue was put on a back burner as both the Bush administration and Congress directed their attention elsewhere.

Beyond the obvious distraction from faith-based policy that 9/11 and the war on terrorism represented, certain other transformations in the Bush administration's approach to such policy subsequently became apparent. The most notable is the movement rightward as the administration rode on the wave of support that Bush initially enjoyed as a war president and the consequent consolidation of his power along the lines of a unitary executive model.[9] After 9/11, the Bush administration's approach to the powers and authority of the presidency was essentially a presidentialist philosophy (one which seeks the aggrandizement of executive authority through the use of inherent and implied executive powers) whose origins may be found variously in constitutional theories of the "unitary executive" developed from the post-Watergate 1970s on. The result is that instead of focusing on creating any kind of political consensus, the faith-based policy under Bush seemed to become all the more a part of the simplistic vision of good and evil cited by Daly, and a pawn moved by the left and the right on the battlefield of the growing blue state/red state culture war. This was compounded by the president's increasingly confused (at the least) and threatening (at the worst) presentation of the policy.

This confusion and attendant sense of menace is due not only to the administration's growing confidence in its power base, but also to the blurred image and perception of Bush-the public servant and Bush-the private man. Numerous commentators note that the Bush administration's dominating and ambitious presidentialism melded well with the man's personal leadership style.[10] Likewise, in the context of his faith-based policy, there often was a blurring of the public president and the private evangelical. And although there have been other evangelical presidents that preceded George W. Bush, no other president had translated so intensely their evangelicalism directly into policy. As Garry Wills notes, "his conversion came late and had a political aspect to it . . . [and it] was a wrenching away from mainly wasted years. [For example, Bush] joined a Bible study culture [with Marvin Olasky] in Texas that was unlike anything Eisenhower bought into" (498). What also distinguishes Bush from his predecessors is, as Wills dryly adds, that he talked "evangelical talk as no other president has, including Jimmy Carter . . . " (498).

The consequent perception is that after 9/11 and, perhaps, being emboldened by his growing presidential confidence, Bush-the evangelical (as opposed to Bush-the president) seemed to progressively come to the fore when dealing with faith-based policy. Consider, for example, Bush's first presidential campaign speech on July 22, 1999, "The Duty of Hope." Here, reminiscent of Gore's speech, Bush clearly outlines a centrist vision:

> In every instance where my administration sees a responsibility to help people, we will look first to faith-based organizations, charities, and community groups that have shown their ability to save and change lives. . . .
>
> Sometimes the armies of compassion are outnumbered and out-flanked and outgunned. . . . It is not enough to call for volunteering. We will keep a commitment to pluralism, not discriminating for or against Methodists or Mormons or Muslims, or good people of no faith at all. Government cannot be replaced by charities, but it must welcome them as partners, not resent them as rivals. ("Duty")[11]

And in the early days of his presidency the resonance between the Bush and Gore speeches was both continued and reinforced. In January 29, 2001, for example, Bush made the following comments at the signing ceremony which created the White House Office of Faith-Based and Community Initiatives (OFBCI). Noting that "when people of faith provide social services, we will not discriminate against them," Bush also made it a point to underline that his administration would never "fund the religious activities of any group," (Bush "Executive"). Three days later, Bush again asserted this centrist vision at the National Prayer Breakfast on February 1, 2001, stressing that our "plan will not favor religious over nonreligious institutions. As president I'm interested in what's constitutional, and I'm interested in what works" (Bush "National Prayer"). Insisting on this healthy, balanced respect for the role that government should continue to play, Bush later hammered home key themes initiated in "The Duty of Hope" speech in his address to Congress on February 28, 2001: "Government cannot be replaced by charities or volunteers. And government should not fund religious activities."

Perhaps, though, Bush's most effective form of reassurance that his policy was not an irresponsible, right-wing, theocratic subterfuge is found in his speech at the University of Notre Dame on May 20, 2001. Here Bush placed his initiative in an evolutionary process in America's "determined assault" on poverty, acknowledging policy successes achieved by Johnson's War on Poverty and Clinton's offensive against welfare dependency (Bush "Commencement"). These examples corroborate the assertions made by all the members I interviewed (Dilulio, Gerson, and Carlson-Thies) of the Bush team involved with implementing the policy that Bush began in 2001 with a consensual bi-partisan plan that respected religious pluralism. Dilulio, in particular, gives a precise timeframe, stating that Bush himself made numerous public statements which plainly reiterated and underlined the centrist position in the first half year after the creation of the OFBCI: "President Bush never publicly-nor, in my presence privately-retreated one inch from these principles" (*Godly* 130).

As we advance through Bush's presidency, though, it seems to progressively become a very different faith-based vision. A vision in which the staunch and reassuring statements made in defense of moderation and in recognition of the pluralism of the American people later give way to allusions to a far more specific American public concerning the predominance of a far more specific type of religion. In the 2003 State of the Union Address Bush declared "For so many in our country—the homeless and the fatherless, the addicted—the need is great. Yet there's power, wonder-working power, in the goodness and idealism and faith of the American people . . . I ask you to pass both my Faith-Based Initiative and the Citizen Service Act, to encourage acts of compassion that can transform America one heart and one soul at a time" (Bush "State"). Arthur Farnsley was quick to point out that Bush gave evangelical conservatives "a wink and a nod." Farnsley finds the nod in the view that "social problems are not caused by institutional defects in the government or marketplace but by individual irresponsibility—hence the solution is to change hearts and minds one by one" (27). He then writes that the wink was "to a conservative, evangelical moral vision of transformation. Anyone who has ever attended a camp meeting knows that the 'wonder-working power' is in 'the blood of the Lamb'" (27).

It perhaps goes without saying that Bush has, like any individual, the right to his personal beliefs. What Farnsley demonstrates, however, is the way(s) in which an outspoken president like Bush could easily be seen as insidiously using (or hiding behind) an allegedly pluralist policy to empower a more hidden, ultra-conservative, and evangelical agenda. Unfortunately for faith-based policy during the Bush administration, such perceptions of the president's worldview were not isolated. Note, for example Bush's second inauguration where in a famously public display religion was not only spoken (in the speech of Bush), but also sung (with the hymn, "God of Our Fathers" and a song, "Let the Eagles Soar," written by former Senator John Ashcroft, sponsor of the Welfare Reform Act of 1996).[12]

It is true that both Gerson and Carlson-Thies offer the argument that in order to properly evaluate Bush, one has to see what he did and not listen to what he said (Personal interviews). Also in defense of Bush, one might say that he was in a no-win situation: if he talked as much about his faith as much as Obama has, he would have been crucified. And when he didn't talk about it, he was accused of being insidious and secretive. Ultimately, though, the problem is that arguments about the "real" Bush or about giving him fair treatment are essentially beside the point, given the strength of the perceived persona of Bush that was so firmly ingrained in the minds of many Americans.

The possibility of checking the growing negative perception of faith-based policy under Bush after 9/11 was arguably compounded by another event that took place on that fateful day—John Dilulio was saying his goodbyes and leaving his post as director of the White House Office at the moment of the attacks (singularly lacking in the hunger for power, Dilulio had accepted to become the Faith Tsar only with the stipulation that he be able to leave after six months—he actually stayed two more months than was planned). In other words, the interest in the relationship between Dilulio, 9/11, and faith-based policy is not only to be found in the central role we have seen that he played in the faith-based story before the attacks, but also in the timing of his departure and what his subsequent absence may have meant in the increasingly extremist, post-9/11 Bush White House.

Dilulio writes in *Godly Republic* that the far-reaching effects of the circumstances which surrounded Bush's odd election have not yet been fully realized and analyzed. To a certain extent, the departure of Dilulio, carried out in such a programmed way, incited by its very nature little or no comment and seems to obscure the integral role he might have played. Though in my discussion with Dilulio, he seemed oblivious to this role, there are reasons for making a case concerning its possibility. Foremost among them is that Dilulio is a man Bush liked, respected and could talk straight with. In certain key ways, they were of the same mettle.[13] Furthermore, the story of his stint as director is one of a man standing his ground not only against immense pressures from Congress, but also from the likes of Karl Rove, Andy Card, Jim Bridgeland, and the president himself. Given the critical challenges faced by the faith-based program of a right-ward drifting administration, it could be argued, then, that Dilulio could not have chosen a worse time to leave.

This is not to take away from Jim Towey, Dilulio's replacement, but the facts speak for themselves: with Dilulio's departure the office of the director the OFBCI was subject to a demotion. In other words, while Towey's position as director of the OFBCI was paired with being a deputy assistant to the president, Dilulio's directorship had come with the position of Senior Advisor ("an Assistant to the President, sitting alongside Assistants Karl Rove, Karen Hughes, Condoleezza Rice, and others" [*Godly* 122]). It is also under Towey's direction that the integrity of the office became compromised,[14] acquiring "the reputation of being a slush fund for right-wing evangelicals" (Wills 502).

Consider also that this cynicism concerning the integrity of the faith-based program was expressed on both sides of the faith-based debate. For example, from the right, the bitter disillusionment expressed in White House insider David Kuo's book, *Tempting Faith: An Inside Story of Political Seduction*, covers this period. In his account, Kuo describes at length and in detail how the West Wing came to cheaply politicize the president's compassion agenda. From the left, an antagonist of the compassion agenda, Robert J. Wineburg, goes farther and ventures the scathing critique that "beneath the compassionate camouflage lay a five-star war plan to demolish government programs, mobilize and increase the size of the evangelical Christian voting-block, shift government money to churches and other Christian faith-based organizations in the conservative-led culture war, and develop a smokescreen of convincing media images and baffling words to confuse detractors" (1).

It is true that for insiders like Carlson-Thies, who were dealing with the day-to-day reality of applying the policy, commentary such as Wineburg's seems, at the very least, counter-productive:

> Wineburg is an important analyst of the faith-based initiative, but a statement like this is outlandish and doesn't help understanding. If nothing else, if what he says was in any significant part true, why wasn't the Bush initiative continuously tied up in courts, easily exposed by any wet-behind-the-ears blogger, and totally rejected by candidate Obama? ("Comments")

The problem was, as both Kuo and Wineburg demonstrate in their respective ways, that the perceived objectives behind the policy obviously led in turn to the perceptions framing the stormy debate concerning the legality of the policy's application under the Bush administration. Perhaps Dilulio's presence as a counterweight to real or imagined extremist factions within the administration and on the Hill could have, then, changed the complexion of how faith-based policy came to be identified.[15]

All the same, it might be noted that the potential impact I attribute to Dilulio in the above scenario does contradict some evaluations of him as director. For example, the authors of *Of Little Faith,* assert that "the hiring of Dilulio was not the best choice and that probably a more right-wing and evangelical friendly director would have been more productive" (197).The problem is that this appraisal seems to downplay the idea of the pluralist, centrist approach to faith-based policy that Bush was supposedly forwarding before 9/11 and that the American public was, correspondingly, favorable to. Perhaps the period in which the book was elaborated (2003) explains this evaluation, as the authors could not have known: 1) that the Bush administration would become increasingly identified with a dangerously polarized nation of blue and red states culturally at war and; 2) that not long after Dilulio's departure, any staff in the White House would have to be card-carrying Republicans.[16]

Ultimately, though, the question of whether Dilulio could have been a counterweight after 9/11 to extremist factions is of secondary importance to what the scenario demonstrates about the events (directly or indirectly related to 9/11) that affected the Bush administration as well as its relationship to Congress. And as a focus for evaluating these events, Dilulio's story has enabled us to establish a framework for understanding the lackluster performance[17] on most fronts of Bush's faith-based initiative.

In light of the impasse with Congress, Dilulio's story helps us to therefore see more clearly why most progress was made administratively, as an infrastructure of government agencies was set up and new laws were adopted. Though, as we have observed, such an effort was open to criticism, it also invited commendation. In 2007, Richard Nathan provided the following retrospective outlining such progress:

> The Bush Administration has . . . extended the reach of the provisions [in Charitable Choice] via executive order to 11 federal agencies. Indeed, the Bush Administration has embarked on an aggressive strategy to use the administrative powers of the federal government . . . [and] has created an institutional foundation through the White House Office of Faith Based and Community Initiatives and companion offices in nearly a dozen federal agencies involved in domestic policy and international humanitarian aid. State and local governments have increasingly pursued similar objectives. More than half the states have adopted recent laws that specifically reference faith-based organizations. And, more than half the states have implemented administrative steps to engage faith-based groups as social service providers. (Nathan)

Whether well-understood by the public at large, faith-based policy had at least become a current part of the American conversation concerning social aid. As Dilulio commented, one accolade that the Bush administration could be given was that it put "faith-based on the map" (Personal interview).

Finally, Dilulio sets off the American public's position concerning a long-running point of contention in the debate, whether religious organizations that receive government funds to provide services should have the right to hire only people who share their religious beliefs. Under the Bush administration, this practice was made possible when, in Executive Order 13279, Bush amended language from previous Executive Orders that had banned various kinds of job discrimination by federal contractors. We will come back to Executive Order 13279 and the hiring issue in discussion concerning Obama, as well as in the conclusion. For now we can note that this right is defended in general by principled pluralists. However, despite their argumentation and the role of principled pluralists in instituting faith-based programs, about three-quarters (74 percent) of the American people say that faith-based organizations should not be able to hire only like-minded believers. In fact, the posture of the majority of Americans reflects the position of Dilulio far more than that of the principled pluralists.

Dilulio himself told me "without a doubt, my position is based on my Catholicism and more on just doing the good works' approach (espoused by CST), just help the people and get the job done" (Personal Interview). Admitting his frustration with the hiring issue, he continued that he would have liked "to just move beyond it and start really helping people more effectively" (Personal Interview). Mouw agrees with Dilulio's take and conjectures that his "approach" is formed more by subsidiarity than by principled pluralism (Personal interview 28 Oct. 2012). Of course, the American identification with Dilulio's position has nothing intrinsically to do with Catholicism itself: Dilulio's take on hiring is the product of a vision which, in the transposition of a religious vision of society into a secular social policy, tacitly acknowledges a more hierarchical power structure than that of principled pluralism. For the American at large, then, it is more a question of behavioral patterns which account for openness to power coming down from "above." Or inversely, for the American it seems to be a question of how far one is impelled to go in claiming the authority of the personal in determining an adequate balance between the state and the private when allotting social aid.

If we consider the religious roots of faith-based policy, therefore, the comfort zone seems to be found in the transposition of the model (subsidiarity) which offered a healthy respect and place for power coming down from above (in the form of the American government). As there are no polls which explain the reasoning behind this position, we may only conjecture that the majority of Americans felt, and still feel this way in order to protect the country against the perceived threat of a possible monopolization of social aid programs by Christian Dominionism (as demonstrated by Olasky). Or, perhaps, the majority position is due to a lack of knowledge concerning the principled pluralist vision. Whatever the case may be, it is clear that the majority of Americans are not prepared to go the whole route of the principled pluralist and that, despite being convinced of the necessity of faith-based policy, they feel there are definite limits as to how much the personal should play in the social.

Before stepping from the Bush era to that of Obama, we can briefly weigh the results of the latest poll that, embracing both presidencies, details the consistency of the above position in relation to the American public's attitude about responsible, moderate faith-based policy. As the United States moved into 2010 (the Pew Poll dates from Nov. 2009) the first and most general result to note is that "the public's concerns about government funding for faith-based organizations—and people's assessments of the potential benefits—[had] changed very little since 2001" ("Faith-Based Programs Still Popular"). Sixty-nine percent felt the threat that the government might eventually "get too involved in religious organizations as an important concern," while sixty percent considered "the idea that people who receive help from faith-based groups might be forced to take part in religious practices as an important concern" ("Faith-Based Programs Still Popular"). The poll reported that approximately half of all Americans saw as important concerns: "interference with the separation between church and state (52 percent); the possibility that such programs might not meet the same standards as government programs" (48 percent) and; that [such programs] might increase religious divisions (47 percent)" ("Faith-Based Programs Still Popular"). The public expressed reservations about certain religious groups competing for government dollars. There was opposition to allowing groups that encourage religious conversion as part of the services they provide to apply for government funding. More than six-in-ten (63 percent) opposed "those groups being allowed to seek government funding, which offered little variation from the 59 percent that said the same in 2001" ("Faith-Based Programs Still Popular").

In the context of general support, the same poll demonstrated that government funding of faith-based organizations was still supported in some form or another by 69 percent of the American public, with 25 percent opposed. Also, as the Pew Forum's U.S. Religious Landscape Survey demonstrated earlier (conducted from May 8 to Aug. 13, 2007), the United States continued to be a widely devout, religiously diverse, and religiously tolerant nation: 9 in 10 Americans believe in the existence of God; 3 out of 4 pray at least once a week; 7 out of 10 say they believe many religions, not just their faith, can lead to salvation; and more than two-thirds are not dogmatic, saying there is more than one way to interpret belief ("U.S. Religious Landscape").

Perhaps the most notable characteristic of the polls was the astonishing and generalized ignorance typifying Americans and their knowledge of the reality surrounding the faith-based agenda. For example, after the 2008 campaign (in which faith-based policy was a preoccupation for all the candidates), and after almost one year of Barack Obama's version of faith-based policy, the 2009 poll showed an almost total ignorance on the part of the public concerning the issue. And most Americans were unaware of Obama's position regarding faith-based funding, with only 27 percent knowing that Obama was favorable to such policy. Significantly, the majority (54 percent) simply provided no answer, while 18 percent stated that Obama opposed the policy. However, the most amazing example of ignorance is that after eight years, Americans knew little more about Bush and the faith-based agenda than they did about Obama: only 36 percent correctly identified Bush's stance.

In the context of a general lack of knowledge about all that is faith-based, we can also note that the question of whether Americans had any idea about what specific theories went into Bush's faith-based initiatives is far from clear. There have been no polls establishing the extent of the public's knowledge concerning the theories, whether they be behind Bush's initiatives, or those of Obama. That this would be useful is underlined by a troubling statistic that characterized the position of faith-based policy supporters in the 2009 poll; despite the pluralism advanced by the theories behind the faith-based initiative, 52 percent of Americans feared the involvement of the Muslim religion in the partnership process.[18] And the percentage had climbed from 46 percent in March 2001. This analysis offers no answer, but as with the above-conjectures concerning the models of subsidiarity and principled pluralism as regards the American people, it does attempt to give food for thought and to underline the necessity of understanding what is behind one's actions and why.

As a final step in the transition to the Obama administration, it is again useful to use the Democratic and liberal Dilulio, in that he embodies the trends of the American political debate as we move forward towards the presidential election of 2008 and the appropriation by Barack Obama (and the liberal segment) of faith-based policy. Dilulio at the same time serves retrospectively to put into stark relief the history, circumstances and forces behind an increasingly polarized debate (in an increasingly polarized economic climate) that ultimately crippled and limited the potential effectiveness of Bush's faith-based policy after 9/11. In short, the case of Dilulio helps to explain why Barack Obama's White House Office of Faith-Based and Neighborhood Partnerships continues to stir debate:[19] it is clear that the post-9/11 and post-Dilulio faith-based policy carried out by the Bush administration remains for any subsequent kind of effort a stigma, poisoning such effort with the traits of a bad pedigree.

NOTES

1. The Supreme Court's five-to-four majority opinion in *Bush v. Gore* reflected the political tendencies of the judges: the Court's conservative majority endorsed the decision while its liberal, Democratic minority dissented.

2. This is a conclusion forwarded in what is often considered the reference for understanding such policy in the early years of the Bush administration, *Of Little Faith*.

3. See for example, *Godly*, 132-33.

4. As far as the actual implementation of the policy is concerned, Carlson-Thies and Dilulio outlined how the OFBCI would work with the Corporation for National Service to progressively apply the plan over a six-month period in 2001. The plan had three bipartisan objectives: "studying and implementing existing charitable choice laws, match-funding model religious-secular or public-private partnerships, and seeding OFBCI counterparts in mayors' offices across the country" (*Godly* 123). Any language or calls for legislation that might in any way threaten the Supreme Court's neutrality principles were excluded from the plan.

5. The consternation of the frustrated Dilulio is evident in the following lament: "Having set out to build on bipartisan charitable choice laws that empowered religious groups to partner with government in serving the poor, the debate over the beliefs and tenets language, had turned the Bush faith bill into a clash about religious organizations being somehow coerced by federal law into hiring gays and lesbians" (*Godly* 133).

6. The following is a description of the voucher system and its potential advantages for faith-based organizations: "In a voucher system beneficiaries choose their provider of a government-funded service. Many believe that a voucher-based program will increase the supply, variety and quality of reentry services available to clients: more job placement specialists, drug counselors, transitional housing beds, and mentors than before. Faith-based organizations (FBOs) may be attracted by the fact that under a voucher system (unlike a direct grant) they may integrate their religious perspective with the federally-funded social service, to provide a holistic approach. Religious providers of transitional housing, for example, need not separate by time or location a group prayer or scripture study from the meal time. As a result, faith-based providers can be authentic to their mission and message in all their programming and at all times. Some believe this will ensure that FBOs can more efficiently do what they do best" ("Guidance for Government"). As far as the history of the voucher program is concerned Daly explains that "The Child Care and Development Block Grant established the first such religion oriented voucher program in the early 1990s, which was never challenged in the courts. In 2002, however, the Supreme Court (in Zelman versus Simmons–Harris) upheld the Cleveland school voucher program that included religious schools …" (*God's Economy* 62).

7. Note that this is a simplified version of a complicated process

8. For more information, see *Of Little Faith*, 168-69.

9. For example, see Stephen Skowronek's essay, "The Conservative Insurgency and Presidential Power: A Developmental Perspective on the Unitary Executive," where he "traces these successive elaborations through to the most recent construction of presidential power, the conservative insurgency's 'unitary executive.' Work on this construction began in the 1970s and 1980s during the transition from progressive to conservative dominance of the national agenda. A budding conservative legal movement took up the doctrinal challenge as an adjunct to the larger cause, and in the 1990s, it emerged with a fully elaborated constitutional theory. After 2001, an aggressive, self-conscious advocacy of the unitary theory in the Administration of George W. Bush put a fine point on its practical applications" (2073).

10. See, for example, in *Judging Bush* (Eds. Robert Maranto, Tom Lansford, and Jeremy Johnson. New York: Stanford University Press, 2009), Robert Maranto and Richard E. Reading's "Bush's Brain (No, not Karl Rove): How Bush's Psyche Shaped

His Decision-making," 21-40, or James P. Phiffner's "President Bush as Chief Executive," 58-74.

11. Consider also the following statement in the executive order which created the office: "The delivery of social services must . . . value the bedrock principles of pluralism, nondiscrimination, evenhandedness and neutrality" ("Executive").

12. The following is a sample of the lyrics found in Ashcroft's song: "Let the eagle soar/Like she's never soared before/From rocky coast to golden shore/Let the mighty eagle soar/Soar with healings in her wings/As the land beneath her sings/ 'Only God, no other kings'" ("Bush Pushes" 17).

13. Bush was of course known, as well as chastised, for the homey and direct way he had of speaking his mind. While Dilulio is an academic with impeccable credentials, he is also a streetwise 300 pound strongman from South Philadelphia who tells anyone what he thinks (an indication of Dilulio's hominess can be seen in his highly academic yet readable *Godly Republic*, where the fact that he can bench-press 400 lbs. just naturally seems to appear in the text).

14. For example, a federal lawsuit (Western District of Wisconsin) by the Freedom From Religion Foundation charged Towey and others with unlawful political activities pursued in violation of the Establishment clause.

15. A testimony to Dilulio's worth can be seen in the president's response to his resignation: "he asked me to at least stay on for at least one more year . . . and then we'd see" (Personal interview). Moreover, as Dilulio concedes, "the subtext was that if I had accepted I knew that I would have stayed on for the entire 4-year term" (Personal interview). White House colleagues and staff also demonstrated their esteem and appreciation. For example, oft-time foe Karl Rove affirmed that Dilulio was "the main reason why, next to the president, that faith-based had advanced at all" (*Godly* 136). John Bridgeland called him "a sage and a saint" (*Godly* 136). They equally bombarded Dilulio with "please-don't-go texts and supplications" (Personal interview).

16. Dilulio states that within a couple of years after his departure, "White House personnel, including my old office, would be told in no uncertain terms that they needed to be registered Republicans in order to keep working there; but in 2001, that would have seemed impossible" (*Godly* 117).

17. For example, in August 2001, the White House released *Unlevel Playing Field*, the administrative audit of federal agencies ordered by the president when he took office. Nonetheless, subsequent effectiveness/application was generally very limited and, as Gerson and Carlson-Thies both told me in interviews, there was a lot of talk and report writing, but not much action. A precise illustration of this ineffectiveness may be seen in the failure of the administration to reach out to the black community. We will come back to this subject in discussion on Obama.

18. "The public expresses reservations about certain religious groups vying for government dollars. While majorities think that most religions or denominations should be able to apply for government funding to provide social services, more than half (52 percent) say they oppose allowing Muslim mosques to apply for government funding. That is up slightly from 46 percent in March 2001" ("Faith-Based Programs Still Popular").

19. For a forceful argument of how American culture may be seen as moving dangerously to the right, see Susan George's *Hijacking America: How the Religious and Secular Right Changed What Americans Think*, (Cambridge, U.K.: Polity Press, 2009). For a criticism aimed more specifically at faith-based policy under both Bush and Obama, see Barry Lynn's *Piety and Politics: The Right-wing Assault on Religious Freedom* (New York: Three Rivers Press, 2007).

SEVEN

New Theory: Obama and Lessons from Life

Before the arrival of Barack Obama, it was generally accepted in the United States that there would not be in any near future an administration that could possibly attribute to religion the importance that it had during the Bush era. There was for many a certain surprise as it soon became apparent that religion was playing an even more overt and prominent role in Barack Obama's administration than it had in Bush's.[1] As Barry Lynn, executive director of Americans United for Separation of Church and State, noted, "Obama in a very overt way does what Bush tended to do in a more covert way" (Javers). Tony Perkins, president of the Christian group Family Research Council, mirrors this perception when he noted that he doesn't "recall a single example of Bush as president ever saying, 'Jesus' or 'Christ' . . . [while Obama] is different" (Javers).[2] However, the most overt, controversial[3] and, undoubtedly, the most important expression of Obama's faith has been his commitment to his Office of Faith-Based and Neighborhood Partnerships. The adherence of the new president to such an approach to faith in government was apparent in the priority he gave to the creation of the office. Moreover, in carrying forward the effort to help faith-based organizations acquire public funding, it is noteworthy that Obama's office was charged with focusing on varied new tasks such as facilitating interfaith dialogue[4] and addressing teenage pregnancy.

Concerning the vision behind this policy, former Director of the Office of Obama's Faith-Based and Neighborhood Partnerships, Joshua Dubois,[5] illustrates the perspective that in all of these efforts "President Obama is . . . being true to who he is . . . There's an appropriate role for faith in public life, and his remarks reflect that. And they also reflect a spirit of inclusivity that recognizes that we are a nation with a range of different religious backgrounds and traditions" (Javers). The subtext is that while Obama was trying to create a role for faith in the White House that expressed his religious beliefs, he was also attempting to diffuse a culture war that had fomented and grown under the Bush administration and to enable a return to a more moderate America.[6] In this light, Barack Obama's approach towards conciliation has been described as one based on a deep and knowledgeable understanding of the compromise and mutual respect between political adversaries that historically characterized the American democratic experience, as well as one which responds to the profound and recent transformations of American culture[7] (Kloppenberg 2). At the same time, H. Ward Holder and Peter B. Josephsen call attention to Obama's clear and continued concern with claiming "the Christian faith . . . as a foundation for his politics" (6). This and the following chapter both evaluate how Obama's faith is consistent with this political approach of creating a consensual, conciliatory, and middle-of-the-road faith-based policy that is in harmony with its era.

In this chapter, "New Theory—Obama and Lessons from Life," we enter the first phase of analysis of Obama's religious vision where the salient facets of Obama's faith are illustrated through a short biographical analysis that centers on his experience in Chicago at Trinity Church.

When framing Barack Obama's approach to American politics in his intellectual biography, *Reading Obama: Dreams, Hopes, and the American Political Tradition*, James T. Kloppenberg notes that Obama's "two serious books, *Dreams from My Father* and *The Audacity of Hope*, . . . have received less careful scrutiny than they deserve."[8] Stephan Mansfield draws very much on both in *The Faith of Barack Obama*, using Obama's personal family history and background in order to explain the uniqueness (at least for an American president) of Barack Obama's Christianity. Obama notes that "My faith is complicated by the fact that I didn't grow up in a particular religious tradition. When you come at it as an adult, your brain mediates a lot, and you ask a lot of questions" (Wilson 135). Mansfield first underlines, then, how Madelyn Payne, Obama's maternal grandmother rejected the strict Methodism of her youth, telling "her grandson often of the sanctimonious preachers she had known and of the respectable church ladies with absurd hats who whispered hurtful secrets and treated those they deemed beneath them with cruelty. What folly, she would recall with disgust . . . " (4). Mansfield then traces how Obama's mother, having had only one brief "skirmish into organized religion," (7)[9] became a self-described "seeker" who ultimately embraced atheism. And on the paternal side, the exposure of Obama's Kenyan father to the west led to his rejection of the Muslim faith that he had been brought up with, and his subsequent firm belief that "religion is superstition" (11).

Already, then, Mansfield demonstrates that the varied attitudes of the principal actors in Obama's life led to a distanced, evaluative approach to all religions. For example, in *The Audacity of Hope*, Obama underlines how his mother instilled in him the belief that religion was "just one of the many ways" (204) that humankind sought to understand and solve the mysteries of life. Further, this detachment was intensified by his family's move from Hawaii to Indonesia in 1967, where Obama was subject to a varied and, without a doubt, confusing religious environment. For example, "because his stepfather was a Muslim, young Barry [Barack] was listed as a Muslim in official documents. Occasionally, he accompanied [his stepfather] to a nearby mosque . . . and prayed at his side for the blessings of Allah" (Mansfield 14). Nonetheless, while in Indonesia, Obama's parents subsequently enrolled him in a Catholic school at which, "as each day began, he [Obama] would cross himself, pray the Hail Mary, the Our Father and whatever else the nuns required" (Mansfield 14). Yet later, Obama entered a public school where he was again listed as a Muslim. It is perhaps of no surprise that on return to Hawaii in 1971, Obama would begin a long agonizing search for belonging as a man of mixed race and unclear religion.[10]

By the time Obama became a social worker for a group of churches on Chicago's South Side in 1985, the lack of any clear religious identity had become highly problematic. This can be seen in Obama's personal account of the search to fill this void, which evokes the defining characteristics of a faith that is at once highly personal as well as very reflective and distanced. Previous to his arrival in Chicago, for example, Obama tells us how as a student he "studied political philosophy, looking for both a language and systems of action to help build community and make justice real" (*Audacity* 206). And his subsequent choice of work was part of the search to find application for the language and systems he had explored. Yet in a quest that is expressed in terms that suggest the rounding out of an incomplete worldview, this was only one step towards what he seemed to be looking for.

If we continue to follow Obama's depiction of his search for answers, it quickly becomes evident that it was also a quest for the healing of a spiritual "loneliness" (Mansfield xvi). Here, moreover, we see that the growing sentiment of isolation Obama felt as he worked in Chicago is presented though the filter of his Mother:

> But my experiences in Chicago also forced me to confront a dilemma that my mother never fully resolved in her own life: the fact that I had no community or shared traditions in which to ground my most deeply held beliefs . . . I came to realize that . . . without an unequivocal commitment to a particular community of faith, I would be consigned at some level to always remain apart, free in the way that my mother was free, but also alone in the same way she was ultimately alone. (*Audacity* 206)

Such poignant counterpoint contained on the same page of *The Audacity of Hope* illustrates both the sincerity of Obama's faith as well as its breadth concerning its expression in society.

In the light of this holistic vision of faith, it is first revealing of Obama that members of the faith community with whom he interacted as a social worker on a day-to-day basis directed him towards Trinity United Church of Christ, the home of Pastor Jeremiah Wright. The use of Obama's experience at Trinity as a reference point for understanding Obama's faith is helpful, first, when we see that this choice made sense for the reflective side of Obama. Holder and Josephson touch on this when they observe that "Obama's faith seems closely aligned with the mainstream tenets of liberal Protestantism. That should not be a surprise: United Church of Christ is one of the standard bearing denominations for liberal Protestant thought. Further the United Church of Christ is frequently characterized as a 'non-creedal church'" (64).

Secondly, while the experience at Trinity was built on (and a result of) an already extensive acquaintance with the role of faith-based organizations in the infrastructure of the black community, it is clear that Obama was seeking the holistic expression of the faith that Trinity offered.[11] Obama wrote: "I was drawn to the power of the African-American religious tradition to spur social change . . . In the day to day work of the men and women I met in church each day . . . I could see the Word made manifest" (*Audacity* 207). Obama learned that fighting the battle for human rights "is not only worthy, it is also a divine calling" (Holder and Josephson 63). Connecting with God and fellow blacks at Trinity helped to focus the sense and the meaning behind the dynamic and effective application of the social Gospel that Obama had already witnessed daily in his social work. Obama underscored this at the February National Prayer Breakfast in 2011, stating that "it was through the experience working with pastors and laypeople trying to heal the wounds of hurting neighborhoods that I came to know Jesus Christ for myself and embraced Him as my Lord and Savior" ("Prayer Breakfast"). And as Mansfield rightly underlines, through Obama's education at Trinity under Wright, he "began to find healing for [both] his loneliness and answers for his incomplete worldview" (xvi).

A third aspect of Obama's faith as illustrated by his experience at Trinity is targeted by Mansfield when he describes Wright's teaching at Trinity as being "born of a history of black suffering at the hands of whites and a hypocritical U.S. government" (xvi). While Obama was obviously formed by lessons learned from the Black American experience,[12] Wright's treatment of black suffering and hypocrisy, and the sound-bites that characterize and make of him such a controversial voice, is subject to wide debate concerning the content and the meaning.

Given all the criticism that Wright attracted to Obama, and the ensuing doubt concerning the president's character, it is worth noting that

Wright defends himself by saying that his critics are completely unfamiliar and out of touch with the world that he deals with in south Chicago. He also adds that what they affirm to know, say or quote about him is totally out of context:

> They know nothing about the church. They know nothing about our prison ministry. They know nothing about our food ministry. They know nothing about our senior citizens home. They know nothing about all we try to do as a church, and have tried to do, and still continue to do as a church that believes what Martin Marty said, that the two worlds have to be together. And that the gospel of Jesus Christ has to speak to those worlds, not only in terms of the preached message on a Sunday morning, but in terms of the lived-out ministry throughout the week. (Moyers)

And this would have been the perspective and the context of the message that attracted Obama so strongly to the fold at Trinity.

The point here, though, is not to enter into the debate about Wright. It is enough to acknowledge that commentators on Obama such as Mansfield,[13] Kloppenberg, Holder and Josephson, and E. J. Dionne Jr. all do an excellent job of contextualizing the alleged exclusionist and hate language attributed to Wright. What is useful for us in citing Wright is to show how Obama nonetheless rises above any such allegations of exclusionism (where even if, as some would argue, exclusionism is a facet of Jeremiah Wright's teaching, Obama's experience at Trinity would have helped to define, then, that which he would not believe or accept).[14] Indeed, the face to face with the controversial teaching of Wright underscores a vision of faith in which Obama demonstrates his adamant pursuit of thinking for himself. Holder and Josephson point out that "Obama's faith contains a productive tension between its communal and individual emphases. In fact, he recognizes that sometimes his place within the community will make even his own brothers and sisters in the church think that he believes something that he does not" (63).[15] We will come back to this insistence on an individualised vision of rationality and the role of doubt when we discuss the relationship between John Rawls, Reihnold Neibuhr and Obama. Suffice it to say here that we already see the foundations of an extremely tolerant and pluralistic religious perspective.

Obama's vision is also one which is fundamentally integrationist, where Americans are brought together in a liberating covenant based on the realization of a common interest and destiny. Reflecting far more clearly the influence of Martin Luther King than the debated messages of Jeremiah Wright or James Cone, the final words of *The Audacity of Hope* read as follows:

> I think about America and those who built it . . . like Lincoln and King, who ultimately lay down their lives in the service of perfecting an

imperfect union. And all the faceless, nameless men and women, slaves and soldiers in trailers and butchers, constructing lives for themselves and their children and grandchildren, brick by brick, rail by rail, calloused hand by calloused hand, to fill in the landscape of our collective dreams. It is that process I wish to be part of. My heart is filled with love for this country. (361–62)

Obama expresses here the integrationist themes centered on the firm belief in the capacity of not only whites, but all Americans to live up to their religious and political heritage. And the theological subtext of the "process he wishes to be part of," and the fullness of his emotion, is reminiscent of King's vision of the teleological unfolding of God in history through a social gospel; a process in which King is "just happy that God has allowed me to live in this period, to see what is unfolding" ("I See the Promised Land"). Speaking on October 7, 2007, during a campaign stop in Greenville South Carolina, Obama addressed the evangelical, Redemption World Outreach Center with the following words: "I just want all of you to pray that I can be an instrument of God in the same way that . . . all of you are instruments of God . . . We're going to keep on praising together. I am confident that we can create a Kingdom right here on Earth."[16] Although, as we will underline, this optimistic, emotional, and exultant call to action is ultimately tempered by Obama's grasp of realism, the profound impact of the social gospel on Obama is nonetheless undeniable.

A fourth aspect of Obama's experience at Trinity is that, despite the emotion inspired by Wright's skill at communicating the Black Gospel and liberation theology, it is revealing that Obama's decision to enter into the religious community was not immediate. Rather, it was the result of a process carried out over many months:[17] "It came about as a choice and not an epiphany; the questions I had did not magically disappear" (*Audacity* 209). Obama did finally make his decision and did make "the walk," but even when he did, the specific moment was revealing. Given the typical emotional form of conversion that, in line with the heritage of the black church, characterized the experience at Trinity, the peculiarity of the event for Obama's is worth noting. Mansfield, as well as Holder and Josephsen, observe the discomfort that Obama apparently felt with the emotional intensity of "falling out," that extreme emotional response characteristic of the evangelical experience to "choosing Christ," and being filled with the spirit that accompanies such conversion. Also Holder and Josephson pertinently ask "why link oneself to a church and then not fully participate in all its rites?" (66). They subsequently answer that "Obama himself seems simply to have had a rationalist kind of conversion—a sense that his deepest beliefs were finding their proper place" (66). In other words, the reasoned nature of Obama's conversion,[18] combined with the other characteristics of the trajectory leading up to it, demonstrate why he clearly believes that there are "many paths to the same place" (Falsani) and why he emerges as an extremely reflective religious pluralist.

The view expressed above is consistent with Obama's assertion that neither he nor the church truly knows all the truth. Even after his conversion to Christianity he writes, "There are aspects of the Christian tradition that I'm comfortable with and aspects that I'm not" (Wilson 138). Consequently, while on the one hand he speaks of his "personal relationship with Jesus Christ" (Falsani) or his "personal savior" in the 2011 prayer breakfast speech, he also rejects traditional Christian views of divine punishment where "God would consign four-fifths of the world to hell" (Falsani). Likewise, Obama puts his confidence in his own interpretations of the Bible when grounding his convictions concerning such volatile issues as homosexuality and abortion. One of the most mediatized examples of this is, of course, Obama's use of the Sermon on the Mount as being far more defining than some "obscure line" in Romans when defending his position on homosexuality. Such statements illustrate that for Obama, the Bible "is not a static text but the Living Word and that I must be continually open to new revelation." (*Audacity* 224). In sum, it is Obama's conviction that "religion at its best comes with a big dose of doubt" (Falsani).

Most analysts of Obama concur, then, that his religious vision is obviously postmodern. However, there is the danger of it being given the derogatory label of "religious shopping," a charge characteristically applied to much postmodern faith. A faith where, in general, reality is relativistic and ultimately constructed by the individual and where there is no absolute truth, theories, or foundations. Counter to this assessment of the postmodern belief system, Obama's faith is one in which he feels that such truths exist: " . . . I'm [not] unanchored in my faith. There are some things I'm absolutely sure about—the Golden Rule the need to battle cruelty in all its forms, the value of love and charity, humility and grace" (*Audacity* 224). As added weight against the charge of an irresponsible, postmodern religious worldview, Holder and Josephsen also state: first, that "Obama's faith practice seems no more postmodern than that of most Americans," and then; secondly, that "if Obama began his Christian journey at arm's-length there is considerable evidence that by the turn of the twenty-first century he had embraced a version of the faith that was demanding rather than convenient" (65).

For our purposes we can note that for Obama's "demanding" vision to incorporate questioning and doubt, as well as a firm belief in the role of faith-based organizations in the governing of the nation, it was obviously necessary for Obama to have in hand, as Carlson-Thies so aptly observed, "the language" with which to evaluate and approach the question of faith-based policy. Although a very different one from even that of the principled pluralist, Obama's "language" is the subject of the following chapter.

NOTES

1. To the degree that *U.S. News and World Report* attributed a "top ten faith moments" in Obama's first, vaunted, 100 days: "From expanding the White House's faith-based office to opening his rallies with prayer, Barack Obama has embraced faith in a more visible way than any other president in recent memory. At the same time, Obama's actions on a variety of fronts, from abortion policy to accepting a speaking invitation at Notre Dame—a prestigious Roman Catholic university—have outraged religious conservatives. The confluence of these two phenomena has made for an explosion of "faith moments" in the first 100 days of Obama's presidency" ("Ten Most").

2. Barry Lynn doesn't appreciate this feature of Obama, explaining that "I don't need to hear politicians tell me how religious they are" (Javers).

3. For a concise presentation of the arguments allayed against Obama, see Barry Lynn's article "Faith, Hope and Charity: Why President Obama's 'Faith-Based' Agenda Must Change," *Huffington Post.* (4 Feb. 2010. Web. 22 March) http:// www.huffingtonpost.com/barry-w-lynn/faith-hope-and-charity-wh_b_450099.html

4. Not surprisingly, this dialogue targets the Muslim faith.

5. For more information about Dubois, see Sarah Pulliam's article, "The Perfect Hybrid," *Christianity Today* (May, 2009): 46–50.

6. Jim Wallis's book, *The Great Awakening,* not only pays homage to this effort, but in fact is a result of it.

7. See, for example, Kloppenberg, 1–5.

8. As Kloppenberg observes, Obama's third book, *Change We Can Believe in: Barack Obama's Plan to Renew America's Promise* (New York: Three Rivers Press, 2008) is rightly considered to be "ephemera" (5).

9. Obama's mother went briefly to a Unitarian church, only because Obama's grandfather "liked the idea that Unitarians drew on the scriptures of all the great religion. . . . It's like you get five religions in one" (7).

10. Mansfield summarizes this crisis, underlining that "The faith that fuels [Obama's] vision is fashioned from the hard-won truths of Obama's own spiritual journey. . . . He was a man without country" (xv-xvi).

11. For a concise description of distinguishing characteristic of the black church in the United States, and their influence on Obama, see Holder and Jospehson, 61–65.

12. For more detail concerning Obama's perception of the specificity of the African American religious tradition, see *Audacity*, 207–08.

13. For an excellent portrait of the complex Wright and of his black liberation theology, see Mansfield, 43–46. For more detail concerning Wright's theology, see Holder and Josephson, 61–65.

14. Mansfield provides a moving description of what it meant to Obama to leave a church which constituted "the longest lasting connection of his life, his only spiritual home and arguably the most defining relationship he has ever known" (64). Though Mansfield underlines that, after experiencing Trinity, Obama was certainly not uncritical of his country, the difference of his vision from Wright's ultimately led him to vehemently condemn Wright's more extreme statements (65). For more information about Obama's position concerning toleration, see *Audacity*, 213–16. For detail concerning Obama's experience with Wright at Trinity, consult *Dreams*, 280 – 95.

15. Regarding fellow church members, Obama underlines their assumptions and beliefs that "I subscribe to [doctrines] that I don't necessarily subscribe to. But I don't think that's unique to me. I think that each of us as we walk into our church or mosque or synagogue are interpreting that experience in different ways, are reading scriptures in different ways and are arriving at our own understanding in different ways and at different phases" (Falsani).

16. "Obama Speaks." *cnn.com.* (CNN. Oct. 7 2007. Web. 8 Sept. 2008) http://edition.cnn.com/2007/POLITICS/10/08/obama.faith.

17. For details of this process and choice see Mansfield, 51–53.

18. Compare this to George W. Bush's conversion.

EIGHT

New Theory: Obama, Niebuhr, and Liberals

To uncover the thinking behind Obama's "language" and his approach, we may first observe that analysts of the president, keying off statements and actions by the president himself, have progressively grown to accept the influence of Reinhold Niebuhr and his usefulness as a reference. For example, in Mansfield's 2008 book, Niebuhr is not mentioned in the index. Subsequently in 2010, reflecting on Obama's open-mindedness to new ideas, debate, and experimentation, Kloppenberg advances in his biography that the philosophy that has most consistently guided Obama in his action is pragmatism. While Kloppenberg said that in his book he "chose to focus on one slice of the president's makeup: his ideas" (Cohen), it remains that there are only 13 references to Niebuhr throughout the work.[1] It is towards the end of Obama's first mandate (Aug. 2012) that Holder and Josephsen argue a detailed and strong case for the centrality of Niebuhr's influence on Obama in *The Irony of Barack Obama: Barack Obama, Reinhold Niebuhr and the Problem of Christian Statecraft*.

Each perspective contributes in its way, then, towards putting together the pieces of the puzzle that make up Obama, while at the same time moving towards a more explicit depiction of the theological vision behind his governing.[2] Arguing that the doubt and evaluative method inherent in the then-Senator's faith are generational, Mansfield, for example, provides insight into how Obama may be considered as representative of those of his age group and cultural training:

> The conversion of Obama, too, defies pattern, refuses to fall cleanly between theological lines. He came as many of his generation do—not so much to join a tradition as to find belonging among a people; not so much to accept a body of doctrine as to find welcome for what they are

to believe; not so much to surrender their lives but to enhance who they already are (49–50).

In an analysis of Obama's speeches, above all the 2006 "Call to Renewal" speech on Faith and Politics,[3] Mansfield equally sets out clearly what will become staples in Obama's call for reconciliation between religious and secular America. More specifically, Mansfield underlines how conservatives are asked by Obama to recognize the central role that the separation between church and state historically played in the United States, particularly "given the increasing diversity of America's population, the dangers of sectarianism have never been greater. Whatever we once were, we're no longer just a Christian nation; we are also a Jewish nation, a Muslim nation, a Buddhist nation, a Hindu nation, and a nation of nonbelievers" ("Obama's 2006 Speech"). Inversely, Mansfield's analysis of the speech highlights Obama's messages to liberals and Democrats, such as when they are admonished; "to tackle head-on the mutual suspicion that sometimes exists between religious and secular America; . . . to acknowledge the power of faith in the lives of the American people and[4]; . . . [to acknowledge that saying] that men and women should not inject their 'personal morality' into public policy debates is a practical absurdity"[5] ("Obama's 2006 Speech"). At the same time, how all this translates into a presidential message for the American people, as well as a method for governing as a president, is yet to be determined. What will be, for example, the parameters behind Obama's admonition for "a serious debate about how to reconcile faith with our modern, pluralistic democracy" ("Obama's 2006 Speech")?

In his later book, Kloppenberg addresses this issue, arguing a Rawlsian interpretation of Obama's pragmatic approach to governing as president. Kloppenberg describes this pragmatism as clearly being the product of: 1) Obama's experiencing as a student the specific ideological upheavals in the 1980s and 1990s that resulted from competing theories about feminism, race, and constitutional original intent which created "the greatest intellectual ferment in law schools in the 20th century" (Cohen)[6]; 2) the similarity of lessons learned by Obama and the young Rawls that led Obama "to share with the Rawls of *A Theory of Justice* (1971) a commitment to the dual importance of individual rights and equality" (140) and; 3) the similarity of lessons learned by Obama and the later Rawls of *Political Liberalism* (1993) where rights and equality are not seen as descending directly from some metaphysical source, Reason or Lockian Natural Law, but rather from the particularity of the American experience[7] and "its history of extending democracy to disenfranchised groups" (Cohen).

However, as we advance to Holder and Josephsen's 2012 book, we can observe that Kloppenberg's interpretation of Obama's pragmatism as president can be seen as problematic in relation to understanding the role that faith holds in such a perspective. To begin with, the thinking of John Rawls (considered one of, if not, the greatest political philosophers of the post-World War II era) is one which moved from an early quest of finding a theological foundation for a liberal and free society to one which was based on a totally secular worldview. In response, for example, to his conviction that individual interest was the fundamental determinant in the establishment of equality and justice within a society, Rawls proposed in *A Theory of Justice* his famous "veil of ignorance." In this exercise of the mind, the individual essentially sheds all characteristics of identity in order to attain what Rawls termed the "original position." Here, the individual will be both objective and unbiased in determining with others the common grounds necessary for the creation of rules and laws that, ensuring justice, equality and protection for all, will contour reasonably the natural inclination to pursue personal interest.

What is of particular importance for our needs, though, is Rawls' later development (in *Political Liberalism*) of this line of thinking into the concept of "public reason," a concept to which the liberal state must adhere in order to maintain its legitimacy. In this light, Holder and Josephson concisely describe how, on a political level, the Rawlsian vision advances that

> politics is not simply subordinated to our private ends; in some respects, citizens have a public obligation to be reasonable, and that obligation actually imposes limits on the lives citizens may lead. This requirement of public reason limits political discourse to the arguments that might reasonably persuade others in a diverse community. (71–72)

And it is in this way, as Holder and Josephson further observe, that "two very different associations, the Christian and the secular, that do not agree regarding their comprehensive doctrines, can establish an overlapping consensus regarding what public action to take" (72).

The question, then, is what place if any does Obama's professed religious belief have within a system such as the one forwarded by Rawls? And how does it affect the message Obama wishes to communicate to the American people? Touching on the heart of the matter, Holder and Josephson point out that the motive(s) behind Obama's above-stated admonishment to the Democratic Party to enter into a dialogue with religious America become highly questionable: "[I]s Obama calling on the left to take faith seriously? Or is he calling on the left to take seriously the Rawlsian idea of overlapping consensus, and to adopt suitable rhetoric?" (70).[8]

For their part, Holder and Josephson affirm the centrality of Obama's faith in his world-view. Moreover, they do an excellent job of tracing the reasons which help to clarify why it is the first interpretation ("to restore the religious left") which characterizes Obama's message about faith and the liberal camp. In so doing they also establish the conditions for Niebuhr's utility to a liberal like Obama, and perhaps for those liberals in general who want to bring faith back into their conversation. First, the fundamental problem with the Rawlsian overlapping consensus is that it is not a "neutral standard. Comprehensive doctrines must be held privately . . . If one believes in God, and if one's experience is such that that such a belief orients one's entire life [as Obama affirms], then the Rawlsian demand that the belief be subordinated to the requirements of public reason amounts to a denial of the most fundamental core of one's existence" (Holder and Josephson 72). In other words, while Obama seems both pragmatic and progressive in the "American intellectual tradition" (72), the pragmatism that Kloppenberg advances as defining Obama is built on a system which proclaims that there are no general rules of human behavior, consequently no absolute principles, and consequently, no God. Obama, on the contrary, as we have seen when speaking about postmodern faith, does advance that such truths exist. For a believer like Obama, therefore, a vacuum without such general rules would seemingly be problematic.

It would also create a dilemma for Americans and their understanding of what Obama means in his stated approach to policy, "doing what works."[9] In this light, Holder and Josephson rightly ask, "Of course we should do what works—but for what end? Ultimately we still require a concept of a great or greatest good" (73). Pragmatism, by itself and considered in a context of simply applying that which works, is obviously insufficient for describing what Obama's professed objectives should be.

In the final analysis, Holder and Josephson assert that Obama's approach to faith bridges the above-described divides seeming "at once sincere and Rawlsian" (73).[10] For example, the Rawlsian, and somewhat cynical, interpretation of his call for faith as being a rhetorical necessity can seem plausible when we read Obama's assertion that failure to acknowledge the role of faith for Americans is, quite simply, "bad politics" (*Audacity* 214) and that "when we abandon the field of religious discourse . . . others will fill the vacuum" (*Audacity* 214). He then goes on to comment on the "rhetorical problem" (214) and the necessity of speaking the language that the great multitude of Americans understand. On the other hand, almost immediately Obama: appends the above statement with "Our failure is not just rhetorical, though" (215); develops the role that "values and culture play in addressing social problems" (214–16) and, then; suggests that progressives must "recognize the values that both religious and secular people share when it comes to the moral and material direction of our country . . . [and that] the need to think in terms of 'thou' and not just 'I,' resonates in religious congregations across the country" (216). The approach is thus premised not only on the difference between the secular and the religious, but on the acknowledgment of, and accommodation for, the place, role, and integrity of religion as a possible foundation for being a worldview and player in government.

Unlike the Rawlisian vision, then, Obama's approach is not exclusive of religion, but rather inclusive.

This is where referencing one of the president's favorite thinkers, Niebuhr, is helpful to gain more precision concerning Obama, his thought, and how he applies it in a faith-based policy. Moreover, study of Niebuhr is called for given that, in large part due to Obama, his Christian realism is subject to a sort of revival in contemporary America and asserted to be of extreme pertinence concerning the issues faced by present-day Americans, particularly on the liberal side.

An introductory comment to make about the interest Niebuhr holds for Obama arises from the fact that Obama's statements about religion being at its best when in the presence of doubt strikingly call to mind the explicit role of doubt in the thought of another great theologian, Paul Tillich,[11] where there is no certainty that in any faith there is the true representation of the unfathomable and infinite dynamic termed "the ultimate concern." Despite the striking similarity with Obama's view, what is useful about our referencing Tillich is that that there is absolutely no mention of him whatsoever, whether by Obama or by his commentators, for the undoubtedly simple reason that Tillich doesn't have much to say about the application of his theology in political life.[12] Niebuhr too encourages a form of moral doubt where the believer questions his/her motivations and pretensions to special virtue, but it is in the correlation he offers between the theoretical and the applied in the context of political action that is at the crux of the much discussed link between his thought and Obama's policy.

It is also because of this linkage that Niebuhr is considered by many to be the outstanding, supreme public theologian of the twentieth century. In the words of Arthur Schlesinger, "Niebuhr brilliantly applied the tragic insights of Augustine and Calvin to moral and political issues" (Schlesinger). His landmark, two-volume theological work (published in 1941, 1943) is *Nature and Destiny of Man,* while his more political work develops from the 1932 *Moral Man and Immoral Society,* through *The Children of Light and the Children of Darkness: A Vindication of Democracy and a Critique of Its Traditional Defense* (published in 1944) and culminates in 1952 with *The Irony of American History.* What is perhaps most striking about Niebuhr is the breadth and diversity of both his interests and his work displayed during the very long span of his career:

> He turned out many books, many articles; wrote journalistically; wrote highly, densely scholarly works . . . He was involved in the politics of the day, from World War I all the way to the Vietnam War. So he was not only a theologian of great distinction, but also a public intellectual who addressed himself to the full range of public concerns and had an enormously capacious mind . . . " (McClay "Obama's Favorite")

The interest that such a synthesis between idea and action could have for Obama can be first seen in a much discussed 2007 interview with op-ed columnist David Brooks of the *New York Times*. Brooks recounts that "Out of the blue I asked, "Have you ever read Reinhold Niebuhr?" (Brooks). Surprising Brooks, Obama gives the first (at least public) indication of his penchant for Niebuhr, declaring enthusiastically that "I love him. He's one of my favorite philosophers" (Brooks).

Already Obama's reaction is revealing for a number of reasons. First, as analysts have noted, Niebuhr is not a philosopher, but a theologian. Perhaps Obama's erroneous identification is just a slip of the tongue by a then over-tired presidential candidate. Even so, it does reveal once more the cerebral nature of the faith with which Obama faces the world. Secondly, and more importantly, it is clear that the interest that Obama professed finding in Niebuhr (whatever that may actually be for Obama) was not just lip-service as it was soon thereafter made manifest in the form of the president's 2009 Nobel Peace Prize acceptance speech.[13] Outlining Obama's conception of the mission of the United States in the world, we might note that the speech also underscores the salient fact that the over-all influence of Niebuhr's vision of Christianity (in the form of Christian realism) on Obama has been mediatized in the president's language and actions in foreign policy.[14] For the purposes of understanding Obama's approach to his faith-based policy, we will see that the influence also has at the same time a wider application than just the president's foreign policy.

Wilfred McClay touches on this pertinence of Niebuhr, not only in relation to Obama, but to contemporary American liberals in general, when he explains the impossibility of imagining Niebuhr "operating in anything other than a modern, Western, liberal environment, where there's a strong tradition of science, of belief in the idea of progress—a society that is in some ways poised on the cusp of a transformation into secularity . . . He was very much a creature of that historical moment and a critic of liberalism from within liberalism" ("Obama's Favorite").[15] In general, then, beyond the synthesis of idea and action, it is this pertinence of self-critical thought emanating from a one-time liberal zealot of the Enlightenment belief in perfectibility that makes Niebuhr attractive to a president seeking to carry on the liberal tradition in a postmodern world. Niebuhr provides an amazingly broad vision of faith-grounded realism to liberals trying to take faith back into politics.

What a modern-day critic of liberalism from within liberalism like Obama gains specifically from Niebuhr is illustrated in the continuation of the Brooks interview. After declaring his interest in Niebuhr, Obama then answers the question of what he takes away from the theologian:

> I take away . . . the compelling idea that there's serious evil in the world, and hardship and pain. And we should be humble and modest

in our belief we can eliminate those things. But we shouldn't use that as an excuse for cynicism and inaction. I take away . . . the sense we have to make these efforts knowing they are hard, and not swinging from naïve idealism to bitter realism. (Brooks)

A first question we might ask is what Obama understands by "serious evil." What is its source? Here, the value of the answer is not based on what Obama takes from Niebuhr, but rather on what he doesn't take. For Niebuhr the meaning and the source of evil is very clear, original sin, and is part of an orthodox conception of Christianity. Obama, by comparison, simply has not stated clearly, as of yet, any orthodox Christian perspective. In 2004 he did state that sin, for him, resulted from his "being out of alignment with my values" (Falsani). However, Holder and Josephson point out the insufficiency of this vision in the Niebuhrian worldview: "For Niebuhr, sin has definite dimensions—and the standard is not a human valuation" (1). McClay adds that "Sin was not just a word that we use to describe bad institutions that can be corrected. Sin, he thought, was something much deeper, an intrinsic part of the human condition, something that social reform was powerless to do much, if anything, about" ("Obama's Favorite").

In general, then, it may be asserted that, first, Obama's belief about sin, until further definition, seems far more humanistic than anything resembling Niebuhr. Secondly, Obama's position concerning sin and evil reflects what seems to be a rather common occurrence among liberal and progressive Christians when confronting Niebuhr.[16] Thirdly, and perhaps most importantly as it sets Obama apart, his stance again shows us the unorthodox character of a faith that results from the "productive tension" between the individual and the communal, the insistent pursuit of his thinking for himself, and the consequent individualised vision of rationality.

Keying off Obama's answers in the interview, a first means for understanding what Obama does take from Niebuhr comes in the form of a question: Why in the face of evil can one's response be only "humble and modest?" The answer first necessitates a brief outline of the role of what are generally referred to as the two lenses or filters of Niebuhr's vision, "paradox" and "irony."

In the case of paradox, Niebuhr sees in the self "a paradoxical compound of freedom and finitude. The freedom of self is both essentially limitless and irrevocably limited" (Molotky 101). As far as knowledge is concerned, then, "the paradoxical self represents the only intelligible means of self-understanding available" (Molotky 101). The paradoxical therefore extends into the Niebuhrian understanding of humanity and history. Holder and Josephson give a particularly useful illustration of such paradox when they cite Niebuhr's conception of the biblical vision of grace:

> Christians are given a gift and so should hold firmly to their faith. But
> because it is a gift, they should be humble, recognizing that they nei-
> ther deserve the gift, nor fully understand the giver. Thus, Christians
> must at one and the same time hold onto a set of truth claims, but also
> be tolerant enough of other truth claims to consider their possibility.
> (Holder and Josephson 42)

It is already clear that a position which acknowledges "humbleness" and
"modesty" concerning human aspirations towards true understanding,
while at the same time grounding it in the necessity to hold onto a set of
truth claims, fits Obama's questioning and reflective style of faith.

The need to curtail human pretention is further supplemented by the
other lens of Niebuhr's worldview, irony. Here, Niebuhr not only underlines the incapacity of humankind to carry out their ideals in society, but
more importantly the ambivalent capacity of the human for the sublime
as well as the abominable. This incongruity stems from the condition
where "humans can see beyond their reach, and constantly try to make
the visions reality" (Holder and Josephson 41). The filters of irony and
paradox lead to a moderating vision of humankind that stands as a bul-
wark, therefore, against the potential extremism of a religious right as
well as a secular left.

In the context of the religious right, an observation by Schlesinger
made in 2006 during the heat of the culture war underscores this topical
interest Niebuhr has come to enjoy among liberals:

> I think some of the criticism by Christian moderates and liberals of
> what we would see as a hyper-politicized Christian right square very
> much with some of Niebuhr's criticism of a certain style of Christianity,
> a kind of revivalism that he was critical of in his own time. Niebuhr
> enjoined the believer to understand that "the worst corruption is a
> corrupt religion." (Schlesinger)

As a reaction to the deification of the nation and the religiously righteous,
naïve pretention of attaining and possessing the answer for delivering
the world, Niebuhr's Christian humility serves as a reference for liberals
in its assertion that a realistic vision of faith still demands self-question-
ing and the necessary activity of doubt when evaluating motivations and
pretensions to spiritual perfection and virtue.

It is also because of this linkage that Niebuhr is considered by many to
be the outstanding, supreme public theologian of the twentieth century.

However, beyond the context of reaction to the religious right, the
topicality of Niebuhr also lies in the concomitant reminder to both Obama and liberals on how they must be proactive in response to the right-
eousness and utopianism of secular liberalism. It is Niebuhr's view that
the temptation to play God in history equally applies to liberal thought
and its pretention of attaining, through the tenets of the Enlightenment,
the perfectibility of the human race. Dionne observes that before World

War II, "Liberalism was easily attacked for soupy optimism about human nature and for self-righteous idealism that had little self-awareness. With the rise of the Nazis and the Stalinists in the 1930s, this optimism collapsed" (31). Niebuhr, a pacifist previous to this period, resigned in 1940 from the anti-war socialist party and championed a pro-active stance of resistance against the despots based on a Christian realism. Niebuhr garnered criticism at the time from fellow liberals, but more importantly left what became one of the most influential visions of the twentieth century.

Dionne continues with the observation that "Niebuhr imbued American liberalism with realism—about the world in general and human nature in particular. He thus rescued the liberal creed from sentimentalism" (31). For Niebuhr, the rosy-eyed vision of humankind's capacity to perfect itself was obviously a dream (or nightmare) that had forgotten the original, fallen, sinful nature at the very heart of humanity, sin signifying for Niebuhr rebellion against God. The Augustinian reminder to liberals of original sin was accordingly expressed through such dark declarations as the iconic, "Man's capacity for justice makes democracy possible, but man's capacity for injustice makes democracy necessary." The "modesty and humbleness" that Obama takes from Niebuhr may be seen, then, as a reflection of this sobered view of what the liberal mission and the state can truly accomplish.

A further dimension of the view concerning liberal ambitions that Obama takes from Niebuhr is to be found in the equally sober realization that the social gospel is subject to the same truncation. Indeed, translating the Gospel as a Christian socialist guide for progress towards greater equality and justice through social reform, theologian Walter Rauschenbusch's belief in the possibility of redeeming the institutions of society and bringing forth God's kingdom on earth was a religious element of progressivism.[17] Rauschenbusch, probably the most well-known and influential social gospeler, advanced that "We have the possibility of so directing religious energy by scientific knowledge that a comprehensive and continuous reconstruction of social life in the name of God is within the bounds of human possibility" (McClay "Obama's Favorite"). In opposition to this pretention of perfectibility, Niebuhr found it "to be utterly naïve about human nature, about the intractability of human nature, and inadequate to the task of explaining the nature of power relations as they existed in the real world" (McClay "Obama's Favorite"). In other words, we again find the naïve idea of the perfectibility of humanity and the need, through Christian realism and humility, to temper the ardor of such pretention.

The limits placed on such a noble dream[18] would seem to be particularly poignant to Obama, given that this reformism, lagging in popularity after WWII, was inherited and reinvigorated in the beauty and soaring optimism of Martin Luther King, the civil rights movement, as well as in the black liberation theology of Jeremiah Wright. The degree to which

Obama incorporates Niebuhr's realism as a counterpoint to what was clearly a fundamental model in the president's viewpoint is open to speculation. But such statements as those in the quotation with Brooks make it clear that, understanding the difficulty of the task before him, Obama is neither a utopian in his hopes nor one to deify the nation with a clear and righteous vision of its mission.

How Niebuhr's truncated vision of the social gospel may nonetheless be said to contribute positively within a worldview such as Obama's comes into play in the conclusion of Obama's answer to Brooks about what he takes away from the theologian: "We shouldn't use that as an excuse for cynicism and inaction. I take away . . . the sense we have to make these efforts knowing they are hard, and not swinging from naïve idealism to bitter realism" (Brooks). While acknowledging the very logical alternative that comes of looking at the world as it is, simple "cynicism" and defeatism, Obama demonstrates here the armor of what may be considered a healthy "realism." Having this kind of realism, and avoiding "naïve idealism," translates into Niebuhrian language as "getting your hands dirty." Although Neibuhr affirmed original sin, rejected leftist utopianism and, consequently, the naïve pretensions of the social gospel, McClay qualifies the apparent negativity inherent in such a position with the following observation:

> [It] did not mean that he gave up on social reform. And Niebuhr was a man of the left and he remained a man of the left always . . . And he believed Christians were obligated to work actively . . . for the realization of justice and righteousness, but they had to do this in a way [where they] abandoned their illusions, not least in the way they thought about themselves. The pursuit of social justice would involve them in acts of sin and acts of imperfection. Even the most surgical action, one might say, involves collateral damage. But the Christian faith, just as inexorably, called its adherents to a life of perfect righteousness, a calling that would seem to give no quarter to dirty hands. So we're left with the feeling that Niebuhr is calling Christians to the impossible and, in a sense, he is. He insists original sin is true. He insists that its probative value is confirmed every day. Yet he insists at the same time that human beings are splendidly endowed by their Creator, still capable of acts of nobility and generosity or truth, still able to advance the cause of social improvement. All of these things he insisted are true at the same time and all have an equivalent claim. So he's correcting the social gospel . . . but he's not abandoning it entirely. ("Obama's Favorite")

After the polarization of the culture war, Niebuhr's moderating thought has, consequently, been forwarded as extremely pertinent for liberals of faith in general, and for Obama in particular. And it is notable that at least two years before Obama was even president, Dionne was already using both Obama and Niebuhr as a source of hope and possibility for liberals to reclaim faith and politics after the religious right.[19]

Given this role of Obama as a focus for liberals of faith, Mansfield helpfully points out that Obama was not only a rallying point for reclaiming "the religious voice of the American political Left" (xv). He was also "raising the banner of what he hopes will be the faith-based politics of a new generation" (xv). In other words, a larger question raised by Obama's faith-based politics is how they are fit not just for liberals, but for a new age of America. We will return to a more general survey of this relationship between Obama and the American religious landscape in the concluding chapter. Here we will simply underline that Obama is a president who was and has been faced with the task of overcoming formidable obstacles in bringing Americans back to some kind of tenable consensus. And in this context, we see that Obama is light years from the extreme evangelical label of Dominionism that, escaping the more moderate Christian Democrat model, came to typify the Bush administration's program.

In addition, as we transition from the theory behind the program to the application of it, it should be evident that while Obama continued the program, the thinking behind the policy differs from the religious theory provided by the Christian Democratic model. Obama's faith is introspective, eclectic, like the man himself. In the Christian Democratic model there is a more doctrinaire system to apply within which things make sense. A system where there is a centrality of God and a filtering down and/or a filtering within the social structures of society. Obama's faith was constructed from the bottom up, as he sought an explanation for the day to day effectiveness he saw as an at-the-time churchless social worker. Compare, for example, principled pluralist Richard Mouw's finding of Abraham Kuyper and sphere sovereignty, where Mouw was looking for a social vision to fit his Christian faith (*Abraham* viii), and the inverse process where the elaboration of Obama's faith is carried out to fit a social vision, founded on pragmatic and realistic expectations. Obama's faith is supple and reflects on and seeks out possibilities with a view to applying a toned-down form of social gospel within government. Specifically, in the case of faith-based policy it can be seen as simultaneously responding to the heritage of the Bush administration while also projecting Obama's vision for the future.

NOTES

1. Kloppenberg's interest in this project began in 2008, the election year, at the University of Cambridge in England, where he "found himself in lecture halls and at dinner tables trying to explain who this man was" (Cohen). Kloppenberg of course recognizes that family history, race and the personality of Obama are all crucial facets that make up the president's profile, but he contends that the understanding of Oba-

ma's pragmatic vision of "deliberative democracy" in governing is to be found in the ideas and ideals revealed in the history of the nation.

2. It is not at all my role here to denigrate the contributions provided by Kloppenberg or Mansfield towards clarifying what are certainly undeniable influences on the president, but given our objective of understanding the religious thought behind the faith-based programs begun in this millennium, Holder and Josephson provide an account that accommodates far more the professed centrality of Obama's faith in his worldview than does, as we well see, the pragmatism advanced, for example, by Kloppenberg.

3. See *Audacity*, 87–93.

4. Obama further reminds Democrats that "we first need to understand that Americans are a religious people. 90 percent of us believe in God, 70 percent affiliate themselves with an organized religion, 38 percent call themselves committed Christians, and substantially more people in America believe in angels than they do in evolution" ("Obama's 2006 Speech").

5. While making this statement, Obama provided a brief account of some of the great historical moments in American history: "Secularists are wrong when they ask believers to leave their religion at the door before entering into the public square. Frederick Douglas, Abraham Lincoln, Williams Jennings Bryant, Dorothy Day, Martin Luther King—indeed, the majority of great reformers in American history—were not only motivated by faith, but repeatedly used religious language to argue for their cause . . . Our law is by definition a codification of morality, much of it grounded in the Judeo-Christian tradition" ("Obama's 2006 Speech").

6. For more information, see Kloppenberg, 37–41.

7. Kloppenberg cites anti-foundationalism and particularism, perspectivalism, and historicism as fundamental influences on the pragmatism of Obama. For more information, see Kloppenberg, 79–81.

8. While contending with the argument advanced by Kloppenberg, Holder and Josephson simply note that Mansfield does not consider Obama's statements from this angle.

9. For more information concerning this approach, see "'Doing What Works' Transcript." *whitehouse.gov*. (Office of Management and Budget. 18 Feb. 2010. Web 14 May 2010.) *http://www.whitehouse.gov/omb/management/doing-what-works-transcript*.

10. In their description of a "sincerely religious, yet Rawlsian Obama," it would seem that Obama fluctuates between awareness and confusion concerning what does or doesn't differentiate the premises of the religious and the secular. Holder and Josephson cite Obama in his 2004 interview with Falsani where, describing how he can use either religious or secular terminology in framing his approach to civil liberties, he comments that "'the basic premise remains the same'" (73). Holder and Josephson then add that "It should be obvious that the most basic premise has, in fact, changed. In *Audacity* he recognizes that basic premises differ" (73). It is worth noting that it is perhaps a question concerning the register of meaning we can attribute to "premises" in the Falsani quote: does Obama mean that the secular and religious are founded on the same premises, or is he just referring to the premise that enables him to speak about values such as civil liberties using both secular and religious terminology? In other words, the subtext of the Falsani quote would be that, while the religious and the secular each have very different foundations (or different premises), there is also the premise (being referred to) of a common ground that, despite the differences, enables the person of faith and the progressive to address the same issue. In short, the two quotes about premises are not necessarily exclusive.

11. For Tillich, "The courage to be is rooted in the God who appears when God has disappeared in the anxiety of doubt" (190).

12. In comparing Stanley Heurwas to Niebuhr, McClay makes a similar comment about the much-admired Heurwas ("Obama's Favorite").

13. To find a concise list of major articles which have recently come out concerning the influence of Niebuhr on Obama, see Holder and Josephson, 4, footnote 17.

14. Neibuhr saw the world through the filter of realism which prefigured the real-politik of a Henry Kissinger. For more information, see Holder and Josephson, 41.

15. McClay further asserts that this breed "flourished particularly in the late 1940s and 1950s [but] doesn't seem to exist, at least in the same form, today" ("Obama's Favorite").

16. See, Holder and Josephson, 52, footnote 43.

17. For an excellent overview which traces the roots of the social gospel back to a multi-faceted crisis within Protestantism (resulting from the "higher criticism" of the Bible, as well as from the Darwinian theory of natural selection), see McClay, ("Obama's Favorite").

18. There is obviously a sort of nostalgia for the social gospel, as it helped to define the volatile 1960s, as well as the 1970s, before fading from prominence in the 1980s.

19. See, for example, Dionne, 77–88.

NINE

Theory in Application: A New Partnership with Americans?

One of the first major messages coming out of the Obama White House was to be simply found in the choice of Joshua Dubois as Executive Director of the White House Office of Faith-Based and Neighborhood Partnerships. Dubois' long association with Obama obviously contributed to making this an absolutely logical decision. Dubois served Obama when he was still a Senator and, subsequently, administered the Religious Affairs Department during the 2008 presidential campaign. Nevertheless, other options could easily have been pursued, and choosing a minister[1] was also a declaration to Americans in general, and to liberals in particular (already very concerned that the faith-based program was continuing at all), about the role that faith would play in the Obama administration.

Discussing initial strategy behind the objectives of what would be Obama's faith-based policy, Dubois stated that

> President Obama and I sat down after 2008 to discuss the work of his newly reconstituted federal faith-based and community initiative, the White House Office of Faith-based and Neighborhood Partnerships. We examined previous efforts in faith-based and nonprofit partnerships in both the Clinton and George W. Bush administrations. We looked at what worked well and what could be improved ("Four More Years" 9).

A particularly poignant example of what could be improved in the eyes of a former social worker from the south side of Chicago can be illustrated by one of the resounding failures inherited from the Bush administration—the enabling of black churches.

This is not to say that the Bush faith-based initiative was intended to target specific religious groups or communities. The goal was to be indiscriminate in the levelling of the playing field. Nevertheless, given the potency of "black church outreach," (*Godly* 45),[2] the reality of working with and through black churches would have seemed an obvious and natural development in the application of faith-based policy under Bush. Consider the specificity of the African American Church's role in the community as a primary vehicle for spiritual, social, and economic empowerment:

> Black churches and religious institutions . . . occupy a unique and unparalleled position of social activism and outreach in African American communities. Black churches serve in many communities as the catalyst and backbone of black cultural identity, making them natural vehicles through which to channel social services. In addition . . . black churches are a central source of neighborhood stability and social structure. They provide a base for social, political, and economic empowerment. Study after study reveals that social mission and activism by black churches are unmatched by their white counterparts. (Black, Koopman, and Ryden 281)

Already in 1999, Dulilio was thus reflecting on such potential when he affirmed that black churches were ideal for an efficient partnership with government in delivering social services where they are needed (*Godly* 43). In the cold reality, however, this effort under Bush was often reduced to being seen as a controversial, partisan means of enticing black voters into the Republican fold. And this, despite the common knowledge provided by polls and commentators that African Americans were among the most open to such policy.[3]

Obama himself concluded an article written in his last year as a social worker in Chicago[4] by "emphasizing the potential of 'traditional black churches,' which contain not only financial potential resources, but also 'values and biblical traditions that call for empowerment and liberation'" (Kloppenberg 33). All the same, it is known that the bulk of African American churches did not make use of the initiative under Bush. For example, The Joint Center for Political and Economic Studies carried out a national survey of 750 black churches in 2006 and established that only 2.6 percent of black ministers said that they had benefitted from the $2 billion a year made available by the program ("Black Churches " 5).[5]

More importantly, it is the reasons for the failure that help to demonstrate Obama's response to such inefficient performance. One major explanation that the Joint Center's study found as to why many black churches did not make use of the initiative was, quite simply, that they weren't able to: "While many of the churches surveyed had an interest in assisting those in need and frequently offered small-scale programs such as food pantries or used-clothing giveaways, most had neither the money nor the expertise to do more—or for that matter to even seek more resources" (Fletcher A19).[6] The study also found that there was insufficient outreach to black churches about what the faith-based initiative actually was: "While three-quarters of the ministers had heard of the FBCI [Faith-Based and Community Initiatives], less than one in three of the ministers interviewed had any detailed understanding of the FBCI or had discussed with a lawyer or accountant the requirements" ("Black Churches" 4). And only about one in six "had been contacted about applying" ("Black Churches " 10).

As both a response to such failure, as well as a vision for surmounting the above-described barriers between government and the churches most in need, Obama reoriented the policy towards the creation of civic and not just financial partnerships. What we see, then, is a reflection of the Obama who, when he was a social worker and director of a faith-based organization in Chicago,[7] "linked arm and arm with the faith community to restore dignity and meet human needs" (Dubois "Four More Years" 9). Where Obama saw that if government and community organizers could be more open to the concept of working with faith-based organizations and, inversely, ministers and directors of faith-based nonprofits could be both open and enabled to reach out to government, the unified effort would result in "a powerful tool for living the social gospel" (*Audacity*).

In focusing almost totally on enabling faith-based organizations to compete for federal grants, the vision of the Bush administration was largely, as Dubois points out, financial and one which the Obama team wanted to move beyond:

> When the federal government looked at religious nonprofits, it saw recipients of funds, and when a nonprofit looked at government it asked what programs it could apply for to receive federal funds. When we began this effort, we thought that maintaining a level playing field was centrally important, but that dollars and cents alone were too narrow a lens through which faith-based and nonprofit groups should be considered. These should be our partners, not just our grantees. Some groups may never desire a financial relationship with the federal government. Others might not be equipped to manage a grant while following important rules. But all organizations, whether they receive money or not, should still be able to partner with us on community renewal. ("Four More Years" 10–11)

The result was that beyond financial partnerships, an entirely new group of programs and initiatives called civic partnerships was envisioned. The change in the name of the office to the White House Office of Faith Based and Neighborhood Partnerships reflected this focus.

To administer and give direction to such an effort, Obama expanded the mission of the Bush era and prescribed four policy objectives on which the White House Office would channel the faith-based program:

1) The Office's top priority will be making community groups an integral part of our economic recovery and poverty a burden fewer have to bear when recovery is complete;[8] 2) It will be one voice among several in the administration that will look at how we support women and children, address teenage pregnancy, and reduce the need for abortion;[9] 3) The Office will strive to support fathers who stand by their families, which involves working to get young men off the streets and into well-paying jobs, and encouraging responsible fatherhood;[10] 4) Finally, beyond American shores this Office will work with the National Security Council to foster interfaith dialogue with leaders and scholars around the world.[11] ("Obama Announces")

And while the administration offered a new focus to the program that was inexistent under Bush, faith groups would, as true partners, reciprocally help to form and develop the policies through their participation in providing critical social services.

Furthermore, in order to reinforce its new policy role, as well as to create a more coherent and transparent system of governance,[12] the White House Office came to operate as a coordinating office under the Domestic Policy Council. Jim Wallis notes that during the Bush administration the "office was totally disconnected from policy, [with the result that] the White House was doing social policy that made poor people poorer, and the faith-based office would try to clean up the mess" (Gilgof "Obama Dramatically"). Obama's strategy addressed (and addresses) this exercise in futility, providing an infrastructure for greater coherence, communication, and efficiency in applying policy. This has also translated into a far greater sense of coherence among the diverse, subsidiary faith-based offices that are now found in thirteen federal agencies. As the Director of the USDA Center for Faith-Based and Neighborhood Partnerships, Max Finberg, states, "Four years ago we inherited the structure, and now we've built a team" ("Four More Years" 19).

Using as a background the unity of purpose described above by Finberg combined with the call to faith groups to become partners in government, consider the mission statement of the Center for Faith-based and Neighborhood Partnerships at the U.S. Department of Education:

Our mission . . . is to promote student achievement by connecting schools and community-based organizations, both secular and faith-based. The Center is part of the White House Office of Faith-based and Neighborhood Partnerships, which works to form partnerships between government at all levels and nonprofit organizations, both secular and faith-based, to more effectively serve Americans in need. The office advances this work through Centers and staff at 13 federal agencies. ("Initiatives")

Hand in hand with the "team oriented" relationship that traverses the 13 agencies[13] and the coordinating office of the White House mentioned above, we also see the horizontal attribution of authority to non-profits which has led to a multitude of programs and initiatives, each as varied as the departments they originate in. In sum, this synthesis gives an insight into how the White House Office of Faith-based and Neighborhood Partnerships envisioned by Dubois and Obama in their 2008 meeting would, in Dubois' words, "seek to create the interwoven tapestries that . . . the president had seen in Chicago: people of faith partnering with government and with public servants to meet human needs" ("Four More Years" 9).

A further distancing of the Obama policy from the financial orientation of the Bush era was underscored by Dubois when, in December, 2012, he was able to affirm that through the infrastructure of partnerships, the administration had developed the means to aid non-profits in carrying out their objectives without necessarily providing any federal money:

> [O]ur job clubs at the Department of Labor help over 2000 local congregations set up and expand employment ministries without a federal grant connecting unemployed folks to work and to hope. Our Together for Tomorrow program at the Department of Education and at the Corporation for National Community Service helps local congregations and nonprofits partner to turn around their local public school without a direct disbursement of federal dollars . . . We have helped organizations around the country have a greater impact on their communities without creating new grant programs. ("Four More Years" 11)[14]

In short, the Obama team has evaluated success in terms of service and not dollars, considering its public servants as community organizers and not just administrators. Moreover, supported by increased publicity directed at successful programs of faith-based organizations, as well as by statistical data,[15] Dubois emphasizes that the team gets solid, "measurable" results ("Four More Years" 12).

Dubois's assessment leads to three concluding remarks about the partnerships; the first three specifically concern the performance of the policy. To avoid confusion and possible suspicion concerning Dubois's claims, we should make it clear at the outset that the performance results Dubois and his team are alluding to are not of the same nature as those which have historically given rise to the difficulties that have plagued research concerning the performance of faith-based programs. For example, social work analyst, Michelle D. Garner points out that "Current FBO policy-related research is inconsistent or absent on multiple counts. Most problematic are service process issues: 1) defining and operationalizing content and dose of religious inclusion among the continuum of FBOs and their subprograms (as programs within organizations may vary in religious content and dose between each other and the organization as a whole); and 2) identifying and understanding the active "faith" mechanism that ostensibly makes these programs different from secular organizations and programs" (492). In other words, while research about the value of the faith factor in the performance of a faith-based organization's program may be an on-going and perhaps unresolvable process, the number of programs created, persons involved, and participating organizations is far more susceptible to being traced and documented.

Progress is being made in this attempt to determine the efficiency of the faith-based experiment. For example, Dilulio provides us with a brief survey of the growing body of literature that documents the steadily growing impact that the faith-based effort has, through various channels, on faith-based community development projects:

> Sixteen years ago when President Clinton got the ball rolling, there was a good deal of empirical evidence, but just enough to hint, not to prove: that the vast majority of urban community-serving religious nonprofits cost effectively supplied scores and scores of social services to people in need; that they did so almost entirely, most of them at least in the urban congregations, without proselytizing; that most of them reached out to people of all faiths and of no faith, and served people without regard to religion, and; that most, in fact, hired staff and volunteers of all faiths and of no faith even when they were not receiving government funding . . . Today that empirical evidence is closer to being absolutely definitive. A forthcoming four-city study, to mention just one, . . . finds that the average, what they are calling the halo effect [a term, balancing subsidies against services, used in establishing the cost-effectiveness of the social work carried out by a faith-based organization], per urban religious non-profit . . . is far greater . . . than even the early estimates of the replacement value of these congregations had suggested a decade ago. ("Four More Years" 58–59)

Such information is extremely positive in that it can only instigate greater accountability. And although the Obama administration has not been responsible for the studies, they do reflect the defining characteristic of transparency that friend and foe of the policy agree is absolutely necessary for any kind of responsible debate over proper government.

The second remark about the performance of the policy concerns the assertion by Dubois that he and Obama have objectives that go beyond the simple doling out of grant money. The point to underline is that "going beyond" in no way signifies that the faith-based program, applied through the various subsidiary cabinet agencies, state-based and local faith-based offices, does not provide funding. Again Dilulio at the Dec. 2012 Brookings event provides a report card on such developments:

> There are those who have asserted that this broader approach to faith-based initiatives has rolled back funding for faith-based groups, and that is not so. While precise estimates await more refined data, since 2008 it appears that, if anything, both the number of grants and the total amount of federal money going to religious nonprofits has trended up, not down. For instance, the Obama faith-based office

worked wonders, I think, in getting the religious nonprofit community up to speed and into competition for certain recovery act funding and, to take one example near and dear to my own heart, Catholic charities and Catholic relief organizations. Catholic nonprofit organizations have received records amounts of funding during the administration's first term. ("Four More Years" 58)

Thirdly, in the context of performance it is worth remembering Obama's acknowledgment of what may be called the "efficiency in delivery"[16] provided by faith-based organizations. Obama's partnerships are a response to the simple fact that these groups have, through the inherent power of their infrastructure both worldwide as well as within the United States, indispensable networks on the ground which enable unparalleled "delivery." The partnerships also reflect Jim Wallis's assertion that, "Nobody is closer to the ground and closer to the poor than many of those who work in faith-based organizations . . . I would go so far as to suggest that the knowledge and perspective of the faith community on issues of poverty is greater than the combined expertise of the department of Health and Human Services, Housing and Urban Development, Labor, and so on" (*Great Awakening* 5). In short, Obama's belief in the necessity of government entering into partnerships with faith-based organizations, and his confidence in the possibility of responsible governance, serves as testimony to the Neibuhrian way in which: 1) he expresses his realistic and pragmatic brand of Christianity and; 2) he extends the envelope of the traditional liberal experience.

The fourth remark about the partnerships (and no longer specifically about performance) concerns how, despite the overhaul Obama has given the policy he inherited from Bush, there are still key similarities. Although founded on a very different religious and theoretical base than that of the Christian Democratic model, we see through its pluralist distribution of authority that the vision behind the Obama version of faith-based policy is very much an acknowledgement of spheres of influence and the role of associational life. Just as with the criticism arising with the Bush policy, the governance resulting from the devolution of responsibility from the government to religious agencies in the form of Obama's civic partnerships could thus feed into the fear of growing interest group power. Monsma and Soper touch on this fear when they ask: "When religious groups and the state are both active in the same fields of endeavor, how can one ensure that the state does not advantage or disadvantage any one religious group or either religious or secular belief systems over others?" (6). In this light, we have seen that, in order to avoid the private interests of lobbies or other such groups, the defense of such devolution must be made on grounds of transparency, responsibility and respect for the law. To protect, then, against the influence of private interests or, inversely, discriminatory treatment by the state, guarantees are needed.

On the internet site for The White House Office of Faith-based and Neighborhood Partnerships we can read the following reassurance by Obama:

> The goal of this office will not be to favor one religious group over another—or even religious groups over secular groups. It will simply be to work on behalf of those organizations that want to work on behalf of our communities, and to do so without blurring the line that our founders wisely drew between church and state. ("Preserving")

For his part, Dubois acknowledges that "Religion and government, faith and public service, [make] a beautiful tapestry, but a complex one. There are important rules of engagement and pitfalls if these rules are not followed. But when they are followed, when the two sides come together focused on the common good, the impact can be dazzling" ("Four More Years" 9). How then to guarantee the possibility of "dazzling results"?

A first and remarkable guarantor of such results may be seen at the same time as a constructive reaction to the former administration's notorious reputation of being dominated by theocratic, evangelical interest groups. This reaction is to be seen in Obama's creation of a Presidential Advisory Council on Faith-Based and Neighborhood Partnerships. It is clear that part of the strategy behind the creation of the advisory council is Obama's all-out attempt to short-circuit any possibility of his faith-based effort ever succumbing to the charges of being a "slush fund," as it was in the Bush era, for interest groups. It is simultaneously an expression of Obama's conception of the political leader as a moderator and arbiter in a pluralistic, deliberative, and democratic process.

Reflecting on Obama's formative years as a community worker and subsequently as a law student, Kloppenberg underlines the specificity of what is behind the president's brand of deliberative democracy:

> Whereas members of an earlier generation of Americans had been taught versions of the nation's history that stressed the importance of individual rights in the founding, Obama from the beginning learned the importance of community, and centrality of obligations, and the shaping influence of civic virtue in American democracy (44).

The Council is, first of all, a perfect illustration of how this vision of the role of the state is applied in the Church-State relationship. Inversely, the Council demonstrates how Obama's vision of state is intertwined with his Niebuhrian perspective that religion is at its best when it comes with a strong dose of doubt. Indeed, as a model in pluralistic representation, the composition of the first board understandably ruffled some feathers and stirred some controversy. For example, one nomination to the Council, Harry Knox (director of the religion and faith program at the Human Rights Campaign, a homosexual activist group) was called "a Pope basher" (Lucas).[17] Bill Donohue, president of the Catholic League, also asserted that "this is exactly the kind of bastardization of common sense that the Obama people are putting forth . . . The whole thing is a sham" (Lucas). Such criticism can be nonetheless considered as an authentication, in a sort of back-handed way, of the truly pluralist make-up of the group.

The first 25 members of the Council (each serving one-year terms) represented diverse advocacy groups coming from a wide range of faith traditions and ideological backgrounds, including Hindu, Muslim, Jewish, Catholic, mainline Protestant, and Evangelical communities. The Council also included a mix of theological liberals, civil rights leaders, conservative Evangelicals, vocal critics of faith-based policy, pro-gay advocates, and Republicans. Also, given the objectives of Obama to target not only religious, but also secular community groups and associations (unlike the Bush administration which focused only on religious non-profits), the Advisory Council has included leaders of secular nonprofits such as Fred Davie, the president of Public/Private ventures, a secular nonprofit intermediary, and Judith Vredenburgh of Big Brothers/Big Sisters of America.

The uniqueness of this endeavour was emphasized by the Council itself: "[Before the Obama administration] the United States Government had never formed a body comprised of grassroots leaders and other experts to assess and strengthen those partnerships" (President's Advisory Council v). Elsewhere Council members added that "As far as we know, this is the first time a governmental entity has convened individuals with serious differences on some church-state issues and asked them to seek common ground in this area. It should not be the last time a government body does so" (President's Advisory Council 120). The Council itself, then, is a living, multi-faceted synthesis of confessional and cultural pluralism. It is also a study of pluralism in political theory, not only in offering to such a group as the Council a voice in government, but equally in the application of its advice throughout different spheres of government and society.

Here it is worth noting that our study concentrates on the first Advisory Council. This is primarily because it is possible, through gauging the seriousness with which Obama acted upon their recommendations, to constitute a measure of the value such a voice had and has in the creation of more effective policy. The report and results of the 2012 Advisory Council are not at the time of this writing available for such a purpose. Also, the focus of the 2012 group, human trafficking, does not have as one of its tasks the question of how the Obama Office should be organized and administered.[18] And this leads us to briefly consider more closely the role of the Council.

In general, the unique role played by the Council is again first set off by the members themselves who, in a preliminary report to the white House, underlined that the diverse nature of its constituent members

translated into an asset in the process of developing their recommendations:

> Some of us believe the Government must or should refrain from direct-
> ing cash aid (including social service aid) to certain kinds of religious
> entities, whereas others of us believe that, although the Constitution
> limits the use of direct government aid for religious *activities,* it allows
> such aid for secular *activities,* regardless of the character of the *provider.*
> As the recommendations note, Council members continue to differ
> over these and other important issues. But members have come to an
> agreement on recommendations presented here . . . Policies that enjoy
> broad support are more durable. And finding common ground on
> church-state issues frees up more time and energy to focus on the
> needs of people who are struggling. (President's Advisory Council 120)

From the point of view of the administration, Dubois serves as witness to the vital role the Council plays in providing representative, pluralist input into the decision-making process. In a retrospective assessment of the development of partnerships during the Obama administration, Dubois asserts that "more than 70 percent of the recommendations
had been acted upon by December 2012" ("Four More Years" 12). In
general, this can be seen in the introduction of the Council's report to the
president where the Obama administration is charged with fostering a far
deeper relationship with non-profits than just funds provider:

> [We call] for new "principles of partnerships" between the Govern-
> ment and community-serving organizations, ones recognizing that
> these organizations not only provide essential services but also deserve
> a seat at the table when reforms in policies affecting those partnerships
> are considered, designed, and implemented . . . The term "partnership"
> should be expanded in other ways. Too often, this term is understood
> as being limited to government grants for private voluntary organiza-
> tions. It should be understood much more broadly. The Federal
> Government often forms nonfinancial partnerships with faith-based
> and neighborhood organizations. These partnerships are as valuable to
> government as financial partnerships, and they are preferred by many
> kinds of civil society organizations. The Government should highlight
> and develop these partnerships as much as partnerships involving fi-
> nancial collaboration. (vi)

The mission, then, of the partnerships as outlined by Dubois to provide a
two way street in communication between government and community
organization is almost a mirror copy of the first charge issuing from the
Council. And, it is clear that the broadening of the government's role
beyond the financial is very much the language of Dubois's description of
the implementation of new policy directives in his retrospective assessment at Brookings. The singularity of purpose between general directives
forwarded by Council and administration, and the Council's later more
detailed work on creating the framework necessary for the application of

such directives, seem to confirm Dubois's measure of the importance the group has played in developing the program.

Specific illustrations of the constructive role played by the Council abound. Returning to the introduction of the report, we can read the Council's assertion that:

> . . . while partnerships in this area are now commonly understood to encompass joint efforts with secular and single-faith bodies, they should also be understood as involving relationships with multi-religious or interfaith entities, both domestically and abroad. Multi-religious or interfaith entities include religiously affiliated individuals or groups from more than one distinct denomination, tradition, religion, or spiritual movement, and they also may include individuals and groups identifying as secular. By partnering with organizations like these and others working across faith lines, the Government can build respect for religious pluralism and freedom of religion or belief. (vi)

Responding to this challenge, programs such as the President's Interfaith and Community Service Campus Challenge were created at the Department of Education. Here, for example, Obama challenged university administrators to enable students of various faiths and beliefs to find communal objectives they could address in their respective communities and, "working across faith lines," find a way of making a difference.

In general, the progress of these programs is generally tracked, with statistics, on the respective sites of each department's faith-based office. More specifically, Brenda Girton Mitchell, Director of the Department of Education Center for Faith-Based and Neighborhood Partnerships, underlines how, in a very short space of time, such programs have had a demonstrable impact:

> So, we've already had over 300 colleges and universities participate. We were given permission to go on with year 2 in collaboration with the Department of Education, the Corporation for National and Community Service, and the White House; and it is some of the most exciting work that I've ever done, to be with young people who are willing to talk about their faith and learn about their faith and learn that people who don't acknowledge a faith tradition still have a heart to serve their communities. One of our exciting examples was from the U.S. Air Force Academy where a group of Christian, Muslim, and Jewish students worked together with a local food bank last year, and over 32,000 needy families were served through the work of these students coming together. ("Four More Years" 28)

Girton Mitchell adds that the students involved in the program "reinforced not only the need to serve, but they . . . built relationships at the same time . . . they were creating relationships with people they might not have ever worked with or reached out to before." Here we have an illustration of the administration's very clear response to the Advisory

Council's charge to create an environment which: 1) gets results through work across faith lines, and; 2) is conducive to building respect for religious pluralism as well as freedom of belief.

A final example of the influence played by the Council is expressed in the extension of administrative infrastructure through the creation of new subsidiary offices within the executive, bringing the total to thirteen.[19] In particular, the demand made by the Council for the creation of an office in the EPA highlights not only the growth of the administrative infrastructure, but also the remarkable breadth of the interests that have come under the radar of faith–based organizations and non-profits. A good example of how the EPA has been brought into the loop of faith-based policy making is provided by Vanderslice Kelly:

> There are 370,000 houses of worship across America today . . . and the EPA estimates that if those houses of worship were to cut their energy use by 10 percent, they could save more than $315 million to reinvest in their own ministries, and we would be able to save 1.3 million tons of greenhouse gases, which is the equivalent of taking 240,000 cars off the road or planting nearly 300,000 acres of trees. So, we identified a very specific measure and said what could we do to get houses of worship to be engaged in reducing their own emissions . . . [and this resulted in the] Greening Congregations Initiative. ("Four More Years" 33–34)

It is clear that in this widening of the domain of faith-based policy, as well as in the innovative solutions that have been proposed, we are witnessing a reflection of the diverse pool of talent brought together in the Council. And as such, it is a testimony to the creativity of both the inventors and participants involved in this creative, pluralist enterprise.

Beyond the Advisory Council, a second guarantee put forward by the administration to obtain results is far less open to accolades, and is the primary source of the contention concerning Obama's policy. It is also, we might add, one area in which the Advisory Council has arguably been devalued. To see the roots of the dilemma, we must go back to Obama's Executive Order 13498 of February 5, 2009. Here, amending Executive Order 13199 (of January 29, 2001), with which Bush created his White House Office of Faith-Based and Community Initiatives, Obama introduced his own program. Specifically, in Section 3, article C it is stipulated that "In order to ensure that Federal programs and practices involving grants or contracts to faith-based organizations are consistent with law, the Executive Director, acting through the Counsel to the President, may seek the opinion of the Attorney General on any constitutional and statutory questions involving existing or prospective programs and practices" (Obama "Amendments"). In practice, this has meant that Obama has: 1) authority over cases he deems constitutionally questionable and: 2) that a primary catalyst behind the elaboration of this stipulation was the thorny issue inherited from the Bush administration concerning the hiring policy of faith-based organizations.

As we have seen, with Bush's Executive Order 13279, faith-based organizations were essentially allowed to hire who they wished in what is termed co-religionist hiring. If they so choose because of their religious dictate, faith-based organizations can hire only applicants of the same religion, for example, or they may reject applicants from the gay community. Supporters of the position, such as Carlson-Thies, advance that "Bush didn't change religious hiring rules, although he did take various actions to clarify the existing rules, which many did not understand. Thus [there was] all the surprise and the strong conviction that Bush must have upended existing laws" ("Comments").[20] Critics were and remain convinced that the practice is wrong and must be, or should be, illegal. Adding to the problem for Obama is a series of court decisions upholding Bush's position and not the firm conviction of the critics. Regardless of whether one can argue that the decisions were reflections of a larger, wider rightward movement of the U.S. (or as some would assert, a "hijacking" of the country by the right), the courts have often upheld the hiring rights of the faith-based organizations. Taking the hiring question on frontally would obviously have served as potentially high-powered ammunition for lighting up conservative reaction to Obama's own faith-based program. The executive order which created his program therefore made no direct mention of this right accorded in the Bush era.

The controversy, as well as the track-record of cases in the judicial system, left the Obama administration in a delicate position of leadership where it had to walk a fine line between what was determined to be or to not be acceptable in the eyes of the Constitution. A possible option for the president would have been to delegate authority in the decision making process to the Advisory Council, whose responsibilities included providing advice on how to correct diverse regulatory problems inherited form the Bush initiative. Obama did put Melissa Rogers, a specialist in Church-State law in charge of the Council, but the Council was never asked to address the question of hiring and when, of its own volition, it did bring up the subject, it was essentially told that this was solely the president's responsibility and had no place on the Council's agenda.

As a result, when the Advisory Council subsequently presented its report in 2010, it remained mute on the subject. In turn, when Obama issued on November 17, 2010, his Executive Order 13559, "Fundamental Principles and Policymaking Criteria for Partnerships With Faith-Based and Other Neighborhood Organizations," which took into account the Advisory Council's advice, the order remained, logically, silent on the question of hiring. Promisingly, however, the Executive Order called for the creation of what became the Interagency Working Group. Chaired by the White House Office of Faith-Based and Neighborhood Partnerships and the Office of Management and Budget, this group was charged with elaborating uniform regulations for the different federal agencies involved with the faith-based program. Months late,[21] the group's report to the president, "Recommendations of the Interagency Working Group on Faith-Based and Other Neighborhood Partnerships," came out in April 2012. It is true that the report did at least address certain sources of contention (as Dubois claimed).[22] The most contentious of them all, however, remained, and has remained, outside the reach of the Council.

The consequence is that the Administration has taken no explicit stance either to modify or retain the status quo in this complicated and volatile area of policy. Instead, it has stated repeatedly that it assesses the acceptability of religious hiring by federally funded religious groups on a "case-by-case basis." Not surprisingly, numerous critics qualify this process as, at best, nebulous.[23] Barry Lynn, for example, points out that representatives of the administration haven't disclosed the standards used to carry out judgment on a case: "Standard-less reviews are usually referred to as 'doing whatever you want,' not a well-known constitutional standard . . . This has meant that a religious grant-seeker could simply assert—you might say 'self-certify'—that it believed its religious practice would be 'burdened' by not being allowed to take government funds and discriminate with them" (Lynn "Faith-based Procrastination"). With little or no fanfare the administration has thus quietly gone about funding faith–based groups in a process where, apart from the Justice Department,[24] "there is no information on how many more of these waivers have been granted by other agencies or whether anyone's 'self-certified' assessment had been rejected" (Lynn "Faith-based Procrastination").

Nobody has been happy with this ongoing process, and there is frustration, both from liberals and conservatives. For example, Maggie Garrett, legislative director at Americans United for the Separation of Church and State, observed that, in general, "Any time a difficult issue came up, or any time it seemed like there would be the slightest burden on faith-based groups in order to adhere to the Constitution, the issue was sort of dropped" (Posner). Member of the Advisory Council's Task Force on Reforming the Office, Carlson-Thies, was more precise about the cat and mouse game concerning the hiring issue, specifying that "[it] was (and still is) the principal question on everybody's lips. When we asked about it, we were told that this was under the authority of the president alone—and then, 'next question'" (Personal interview 19 Feb. 2010).

Possible explanations for the delay tactics of the administration are without doubt multi-faceted. For example, Dilulio confided that he believes this delay by Obama is open-ended and that the president will never provide any kind of decision concerning the hiring issue: "He's in a can't-win scenario. If, for example, he decided that religious groups can't hire who they want, he'd open a powder keg—it's volatile. He'd alienate a very powerful part of the population [and] would provide a rallying point for opposition" (Personal interview). Obama's strategy is not at all indecision, then, but rather a deliberate policy. At the Dec. 2012 Brookings conference, Lynn made a similar assertion after Dubois stated that the issue was entirely unresolved: "Although there have been no formal changes, there have been at least nine waivers granted by the Department of Justice to allow what some might call preferential [treatment] — so that there is a policy. It may not be formal but sometimes inaction leads to a policy" ("Four More Years" 47).

Beyond contemplating a certain (perhaps cynical) political acumen, we are left to wonder how the Obama realpolitik concerning the religious hiring issue is also consistent with Obama's vision of the role of the political leader and of compromise. As references for this vision, we can note that in a declaration concerning the vocation of the politician, Obama affirmed that, "Politics, like science, depends on our ability to persuade each other of common aims based on a common reality. Moreover, politics (unlike science) involves compromise, the art of the possible" (*Audacity* 219). Revealingly Obama immediately adds that in the case of religion there can be, by definition, no compromise: "Followers are expected to live up to God's edicts, regardless of the consequences" (*Audacity* 219). As a result, he draws the conclusion that "To base our policy making on such commitments would be a dangerous thing" (*Audacity* 219–20). Obama thus specifies the necessary conditions for finding common ground between the political and the religious in a deliberative, pluralistic democracy: "the religiously motivated [must] translate their concerns into universal, rather than religion–specific, values. It requires that their proposals must be subject to argument and amenable to reason . . . " (*Audacity* 219).

While the above view on the political leader and compromise obviously echoes the thought of John Rawls, we saw in the last chapter that Obama's approach to faith bridges numerous divides and seems, as Holder and Josephson observe, both Rawlsian and sincere. In this light, we have seen, for example, that both as a believer and as a politician, Obama is aware that it is absurd to assert that people will not inject their personal morality into public policy. Curiously, then, Obama's obscure "policy" concerning the hiring issue may be the result of an unresolvable (or "unbridgeable") conflict that he sees, in this particular case, between the dictates of faith and the tenets of Rawls. The subtext of Obama's approach to hiring would reveal his sentiment, then, that at least up to now he has not found any possibility, or means, for communicating through secular values and establishing the common ground needed for compromise on the issue. Whatever the case may be, the impasse on the hiring issue and the lack of a constructive compromise would seem a glaring failure of Obama to fulfill successfully his self-defined role of an effective politician

In defense of Obama, it is worth noting Kloppenberg's insightful observation that "the president's philosophical pragmatism assumes that change emerges over decades"[25] (Cohen). Perhaps this is the best that Obama feels he can do at this particular time and place and, in his eyes, the lack of any solution is in fact the most viable of all possible compromises. Moreover, this hypothesis receives reinforcement from the concomitant policy of creating partnerships in which financing (and taxpayers' money) is no longer an issue. In other words, the creation of such partnerships indicates the readiness on the part of the administration to circumvent the controversy altogether.

Of course it can be argued that this inaction should also be seen against the backdrop of other more pressing concerns, such as the economy, health care, or foreign policy, which all have higher priority on the list of things to address. Nevertheless, it is clear that Obama's faith-based policy has received such precise care and attention from both the president and his administration that the hypothesis which simply dismisses the impasse as a side-effect of distraction is not really tenable. On the contrary, with the onset of Obama's re-election campaign the necessity of keeping a status quo became an increasingly obvious strategy.[26] And in a sense, Obama was fortunate that in the 2012 presidential campaign against Romney, it was not in the interest of either candidate to have the hiring issue on their respective agendas.[27]

Now that Obama has been re-elected, there is, however, the possibility that something will finally be done. This possibility is comforted first of all by the departure in February 2013 of Joshua Dubois. Despite his multiple talents, particularly in providing vision to the faith community, Dubois made little or no progress for his Office in the general field of First Amendment issues and, more specifically, in the hiring issue. Whether this was in fact a negative for the Obama administration is, as we have seen, very much open to debate. Nonetheless, it remains that under Dubois' watch, the policy continued (as he admitted in December 2012) "as it was before" ("Four More Years" 48).

The possibility that something will eventually be done to resolve these legal issues is also presaged (or at least suggested) by the choice of his replacement, Melissa Rogers. As one writer observed, "Rogers comes to the post after serving in several positions at the intersection of religion and public policy" (pcusa.org). More importantly, Rogers brings to the Office a lot of know-how in her specialty. Until her appointment in March 2013, Rogers was director of Wake Forest University Divinity School's Center for Religion and Public Affairs. A highly active, nonresident senior fellow at Brookings Institution (for example, she co-chaired the December 17 Conference), Rogers, like Dubois a Baptist, has held positions such as associate general counsel of the Baptist Joint Committee on Public Affairs, executive director of the Pew Forum on Religion and Public Life, and board member of the Public Religion Research Institute. And finally, Rogers is no stranger to the White House, having chaired the first Advisory Council for Obama.

Beyond her expertise, Rogers is a particularly interesting choice, given her approach to co-religionist hiring. Speaking in 2011 she stated that "While I believe religious organizations should have full freedom to make religious calls regarding jobs subsidized by tithes and offerings . . . when government-funded jobs are involved, I believe the calculus changes" (pcusa.org). On the other hand, she is well known for having a centrist approach to controversial issues, for having a preoccupation with preserving and protecting the integrity of faith-based organizations in their dealings with government, and for being a consummate problem-solver, moderator, and consensus-builder. In general, then, her appointment was well received by all. It will therefore be extremely interesting to see if the Obama administration does something more radical and defining in the second term as far as adhering to promises made long-ago about resisting any funding for faith-based organizations that discriminate in their hiring. Obviously, this remains to be tested. Yet just as obviously, it is clear that it is in some way on the radar.

A first of two concluding remarks reflects a general objective of this text, which is to demonstrate the interest to be found in possessing knowledge of the religious theory behind faith-based policy. As a means for rounding off the study, it is useful to note the interest that such knowledge may represent to the actors themselves. An interchange at the Brookings event provides a first demonstration of this when Carlson-Thies responds to the question of whether issues such as co-religionist hiring are really that important:

> Well, let me just say one thing about . . . [why there is], despite all the common ground . . . so much controversy about a few things? Well, you know, you don't fight over the things that you all agree on, but important things in which there are some disagreement. [And] . . . if these issues get put on the table, I guess people need to take a stand and fight for what they think is legitimate freedom. And that is why it is preoccupy[ing]. ("Four More Years" 84–85)

Here, Carlson-Thies is in fact not only referring to legitimate legal rights he argues are supported by the Civil Rights Act of '64, the Religious Freedom Restoration Act, and multiple court cases, but to a legitimacy defined within his principled pluralism. Consider again that his is a vision in which

> The flow ought to be bottom-up rather than top-down in the relationship between government and the private organizations that provide assistance to distressed and poor families in communities. The Federal Government should assist the good work already being accomplished by civil society organizations and not see them simply as cheaper tools to do what the government itself wants to do. ("Four More Years" 75)

To speak metaphorically, for Carlson-Thies, the principled pluralist, his house is built from the bottom up and the over-all integrity of its architecture is dependent on the rightful power of the spheres (or pillars) at its base such as the family, the church and associational life. Without the recognition that the delegation of power is upwards, the whole system is at stake.

In application Mouw demonstrates the importance of issues such as co-religionist hiring, when he notes that potential candidates for Fuller Seminary have to take an oath concerning their values and their faith. But, as students, some will be receiving federal money in the form of grants (Personal interview 28 Oct. 2012). In other words, while at Fuller they are not choosing a potential worker but rather a student, the basic dynamic of the question concerning discrimination along co-religionist grounds remains the same. The "importance" of the questions is, as a result, enough to lead Mouw to a rather bleak pessimism about the policy ever being anything that he will not feel threatened by. The question concerning "importance" raised at Brookings is, therefore, rather consternating.

All the more consternating is that the lack of understanding between leaders gathered at Brookings does not seem to be an isolated event. Even John Dilulio commented that

> I actually do not see the tension between "subsidiarity" and "princi-pled pluralism" as such, maybe because I understand the former as requiring one to be neither addicted to the state nor allergic to it, and the latter as another term for religious pluralism (Madison's "multiplic-ity of sects"). But I am probably not using the concepts as others do or as experts do. ("New Developments")

As we have argued, there can be inherently important tensions between the two (for example, as we have seen, principled pluralists are apt to be more militant about guarding the upward delegation of power than those formed in the school of subsidiarity). In all fairness to Dilulio, he did note that more telling differences might exist when he deferred to "special-ists." The question is, though, who then are the specialists when it comes to faith-based policy? Perhaps, what Dilulio illustrates is that great minds with great aspirations have agendas that may somehow cloud useful perceptions about the religious theory being expressed in their col-league's actions. All the same, on the positive side, we can underscore yet a further value to be attributed to the creation of a renewable Advisory Council: With its sheer diversity, it will constitute a forum that will both cultivate and necessitate a clearer understanding of what otherwise might seem amongst the actors to be unfathomable positions.

As a second concluding remark, we might note that for supporters of faith-based policy, contention is not the defining term in the narrative of the story, but rather continuation. At the Brookings event, for example, backers repeatedly extolled the longevity of the experiment, despite the obstacles it has had to face. A striking example of this is again found with

Carlson-Thies when, just after his statement defending his rights, he immediately adds, "But I think it is really important for the public to see in these partnerships all the things that are going on and all the things that go right, and not just think about the isolated things that are controversial" ("Four More Years" 85).

Dilulio provides an entertainingly cryptic, yet enlightening general appraisal of this resilience:

> There are, I am sure, many differences, but the headline really is still that a Democrat not only kept, but in many tangible ways expanded the GOP-created White House Office of Faith-Based and Community Initiatives/Neighborhood Partnerships, kept most policies and protocols in place, and so forth. Those similarities trump any and all differences: Where is the Clinton Gore "reinventing government" operation today? Gone on GWB's first day. Where are several other GWB EEOB (The Eisenhower Executive Office Building) offices and projects? Gone on Obama's first day. That is as it generally is with presidential transitions even from one president to another of the same party. Only the OMB, the NSA, the CEA and such persist over time. And now "faith based." ("New Developments")

Dilulio's assessment is useful in that it can be taken in two ways. Understood retrospectively, it highlights the resilience of faith-based policy, with the subtext being (as implied by the prompting of such a qualification) that the policy is still experimental. Yet, when Obama's term is up, "faith-based" will have been with us in one form or another for two decades. Moreover, it will continue in all likelihood to enjoy the approbation of the wide majority of Americans. Consider then, that much of the weaponry employed in one of the greatest landmarks in American social history, the aptly named Great Society, was shot to pieces 17 years after Johnson's 1964 declaration of war on poverty. Faith-based policy is guaranteed 20 years and is open-ended. Understood in this context, the "headline" or key idea to retain in Dilulio's message is that faith-based policy has gone beyond the stage of simply being a resilient experiment and that it is becoming, or has become, a fixture in American government and governance. As Carlson-Thies's recent historical analyses attest to, such policy is now presented within the framework of Versions I, II and III: Version I corresponding to the policy during the Clinton era, II the Bush era, and III, the present day Obama administration ("Faith-based" 945–47).

Despite the succession of theories behind the policy, whether it be principled pluralism, subsidiarity, or Obama's brand of pluralism, we have been witness to a common fixity of intent as to the continued application of the policy. And ultimately, with their vague notions of what comprises the thought behind the policy, it will be up to Americans at some point to gain an awareness that enables them to situate themselves accordingly.

NOTES

1. Before working with Obama, Dubois was associate pastor at a church in Cambridge, Massachusetts. Dubois has a Master's in public affairs from Princeton University.

2. Dilulio adds that "Black Americans are in many ways the most religious people in America. Some 82 percent of blacks (versus 67 percent of whites) are church members; 82 percent of blacks (versus 55 percent of whites) say that religion is "very important in their life." Eighty-six percent of blacks (versus 60 percent of whites) believe that religion "can answer all or most of today's problems" (*Godly* 43).

3. For example, Robert Wuthnow observes that, along with evangelicals, blacks in the 2000 election "were the most prominent supporters of government funding for faith-based organizations, and in 2004, the percentage of black voters for Bush increased significantly, and clergy of some of the nation's largest black churches avidly supported faith-based initiatives" (301).

4. See Obama's article, "Why organize? Problems and Promise in the Inner-City," *Illinois Issues*, Aug. & Sept. 1988. Springfield: University of Illinois at Springfield: 40–42.

5. The Study also provided the following detail: "Churches in the Northeast were more interested in participating than those in other areas of the country . . . and churches with progressive theologies and socially liberal congregations were more interested in participating than conservative churches" ("Black Churches" 4). The surprising finding was that "churches in 'blue states'— i.e., states won by Gore in 2000 and Kerry in 2004 — were more likely to have received FBCI grants than those in 'red states'— i.e., states won by Bush in 2000 and 2004. Churches in New Jersey and New York led the list of recipients" ("Black Churches" 5).

6. The survey found that "Half the churches in this study that provided revenue estimates had yearly revenue of less than $250,000, and only 12 percent of the churches in the study had yearly revenue in excess of $1 million. Twenty-eight percent had revenue of less than $100,000" ("Black Churches " 2–3).

7. The Developing Communities Project was funded by the Catholic Campaign for Human Development. It consisted of church-based social aid programs around inner-city Catholic parishes in Chicago's south side.

8. The following is detail from the site of The Office of Faith-based and Neighborhood Partnerships: "President Obama is intent on engaging community groups as an integral part of our economic recovery and poverty reduction. The American Recovery and Reinvestment Act created new opportunities for community groups to participate in the recovery. The White House Office of Faith-based and Neighborhood Partnerships works within government to ensure a role for community groups in grant opportunities created by the Recovery Act. In addition to making sure that community groups are aware of opportunities to apply for funding, this Office identifies ways to promote fiscal and civic partnerships with all sectors and all levels of government to make poverty a burden fewer have to bear when the recovery is complete" ("Strengthening the Role").

9. Detail from the site: "The Office of Faith-based and Neighborhood Partnerships partners with the White House Council on Women and Girls to explore how the federal government can support women and children, reduce unintended pregnancies, support maternal and child health and reduce the need for abortion" ("Reducing).

10. Detail from the site: "President Obama has been of our nation's leaders on issues related to responsible fatherhood. The President knows firsthand the power that fathers can have in the lives of their children, and the challenges families and communities face without committed fathers . . . For these reasons, President Obama has started a National Conversation on Responsible Fatherhood and Strong Communities and made the issue of fatherhood and at-risk youth one of the Office of Faith-Based and Neighborhood Partnerships' four key priorities. The Office of Faith-based

and Neighborhood Partnerships is helping to coordinate the Federal Government's fatherhood policy, and has launched a national fatherhood tour to hear directly from local communities about how we can come together to encourage personal responsibility and strengthen our nation's families" ("Promoting Responsible Fatherhood").

11. Detail from the site: "President Obama is dedicated to fostering interfaith dialogue, cooperation and understanding. One of the priorities of the Office of Faith-based and Neighborhood Partnerships is to create opportunities for interreligious cooperation. To do this, this Office works with offices and programs throughout the Federal Government, including the National Security Council, Department of State, U.S. Agency for International Development and Corporation for National and Community Service to foster dialogue and cooperation at home and around the globe" ("Promoting Interfaith Dialogue").

12. The office has from the first days of its existence strived to placate its secular critics by pledging greater accountability. For example, in 2009 Dubois noted that "We're not judging success by the amount of money that flows out, but by how we're helping those most in need: the number of folks who received mortgage counselling or have been trained for jobs" (Pulliam "The Perfect Hybrid" 48).

13. The White House site provides the following detail: "The White House Office of Faith-based and Neighborhood Partnerships coordinates [13] Federal Centers for Faith-based and Community Initiatives. Each Center forms partnerships between its agency and faith-based and neighborhood organizations to advance specific goals. For example, the Department of Labor (DOL) Center forms partnerships between DOL and community-based groups to better integrate those groups in job training and workforce development programs. The Department of Homeland Security (DHS) Center helps to link DHS with community-based groups to address disaster response. Similar efforts are being implemented through Centers at the Departments of Agriculture, Commerce, Education, Health and Human Services, Housing and Urban Development, Justice, and Veterans Affairs as well as the Small Business Administration, Corporation for National and Community Service and U.S. Agency for International Development" ("About").

14. Dubois adds that "I could go on and on and on from our work on youth violence at the Department of Justice to our efforts at the Small Business Administration to provide access to capital through faith communities; our work at the Department of Housing and Urban Development on foreclosure prevention to our work at the Department of Agriculture to help feed hungry kids in the summertime; our efforts at HHS to connect health systems to congregations to improve public health to our team at EPA helping to green congregations; from the Veterans Administration to the U.S. Agency for International Development to the Department of Commerce and beyond. These civic partnerships work. They help avoid legal pitfalls. They produce measurable results. And they change lives" ("Four More Years" 11–12).

15. For example, on any of the department sites, one can find information and updates concerning various programs. All the same, there is room for improvement here as specific data that would be of great interest is not readily available. For example, the question of providing of recent statistics concerning the participation of black churches does not seem to be addressed by the centers. Such vital research and information is left, therefore, to organizations such as the Joint Center for Political and Economic Studies that carried out the 2006 survey.

16. The term was actually employed by Richard Mouw in an interview I had with him (Personal Interview 30 April 2008).

17. For more critical commentary, see Fred Lucas' "Obama Names Pope Basher to Faith-Based Initiative Board." *cnsnews.com*. (CNS. 6 April.2009. Web. 7 Sept.) http://cnsnews.com/news/article/obama-names-pope-basher-faith-based-initiative-board.

18. The Senior Policy Advisor for the Office of Faith-Based and Neighborhood Partnerships, Mara Vanderslice Kelly provides detail concerning the vastness of the issues addressed by the first Council: [W]e brought together over 80 faith-based and nonprofit leaders, which I had to coordinate, and if you can imagine all the different

thoughts and perspectives. It was quite a task but one that I think has truly been one of the greatest honors of my life to help work with such an amazing wealth of knowledge, of people that came together to help advise the federal government really in a new way. And in that first inaugural committee, there were six different task forces that literally almost spanned the scope of issues that you could think of to bring faith and community groups together to advise government. And they included how we might reform the legal and constitutional footing of our office; how we could better engage faith communities and the government to lift up poverty as a fundamental moral issue and concern of those at the margins as one of the most important things and priorities that the faith-based initiative can put forward. It challenged us to move into thinking about religion in global affairs, interfaith and interreligious dialog in action. And to talk about global poverty and the environment . . . [T]he task force on the legal reforms literally provided the blueprint for the President's Executive Order and the guiding of work that has come since that, so it truly made an impact" ("Four More Years" 32).

19. Federal centers for the Faith-based and Neighborhood Partnerships are found in: the U.S Department of Health and Human Services (HHS); the U.S. Department of Commerce; the U.S. Department of Housing and Urban Development (HUD); the U.S. Department of Veterans Affairs (VA); the U.S. Department of Agriculture; the U.S. Department of Homeland Security (DHS); the U.S. Agency for International Development (USAID); the U.S. Department of Education; the Small Business Administration; the U.S. Department of Labor; the U.S. Department of Justice; the Environmental Protection Agency; and the Corporation for National and Community Service.

20. Carlson-Thies pursues that "Bush changed the rules that apply to federal contracts, not grants, to permit religious hiring. The non-discrimination rules that apply to contracts (which are mainly used to provide goods and services to the federal government, not to families, persons, or communities) have historically been promulgated by presidents, not Congress" ("Comment").

21. The delay was generally seen as part of a calculated, political move to avoid making the suggestions public during the earlier controversy brought on by the HHS mandate for contraception coverage. Council member Nathan Diament, public affairs director for the Union of Orthodox Jewish Congregations, observed that the administration was "dealing with a political fight and they had to do messaging on religion and state and didn't want to muddle their message" (Silk).

22. For example, under the Bush administration there were few or no avenues for recipients of services from a faith-based organization when they wished to contest the religious character of the service provider. Executive Order 13559 requires the service provider to inform beneficiaries in general about the right to having alternative providers and, specifically, to refer those who are dissatisfied with such a provider.

23. Carlson-Thies suggests that the process is mislabeled rather than nebulous: "When a federal funding program includes no specific ban on religious hiring, the Obama administration, like the Bush administration, does not ban religious groups that hire on a religious basis from participating. When the program does ban religious hiring, the Obama administration, again like the Bush administration, decides on a "case-by-case basis" whether the organization can get the funds. This determination involves the Religious Freedom Restoration Act, signed into law by President Clinton in 1993, which prevents the government from imposing a substantial burden on a religious organization—such as requiring the organization to abandon its religious hiring practices in order to receive the federal dollars—unless a vital federal interest is involved and there is no other way to protect that interest. Banning the group cannot be a vital governmental interest since so many other federal funding programs have no such ban. But this is a case-by-case process that requires the religious organization to certify the importance of religious hiring and of its participation in the federal program" ("Comments").

24. The Justice Department "has acknowledged it affirmatively permitted nine grantees to use religion to discriminate in 2009 alone" (Lynn "Faith-based Procrastination").

25. As differentiated from the kind of "vulgar pragmatism practiced by politicians looking only for expedient compromise" (Cohen).

26. Considering the absence of any resolution to the impasse, Lynn observes that "the administration didn't want to resolve the hiring issue in the midst of a campaign where every opponent of the president had declared him the lead general in some completely nonexistent 'war on religion'" (Lynn "Faith-based Procrastination").

27. The absence of the faith-based debate, particularly as regards Romney's agenda, was one of the major issues addressed in the panel discussion, "Religion and Politics: Faith, Democracy, and American Public Life," between John Dilulio, E.J. Dionne, Jane Eisner, and Sarah Barringer-Gordon at the National Museum of American Jewish History, Philadelphia, Oct. 17, 2012.

TEN

Obama, Faith-Based Policy, and "the Center"

In his 1995 book, *Claiming the Center*, Jack Rogers made the assertion that "most modern Americans are neither conservative nor liberal. They have been influenced both by conservative values and by liberal insights so that they are clustered somewhere in the center" (xvi). It is true that Rogers made this statement before September 11 and the subsequent profound divisiveness of the Bush administration's blue state, red state America. All the same, if Rogers' claim that Americans tend to "cluster in the center" has, after the Bush years, any renewed value with the Obama administration, the question is what "the center" means.[1]

One way of considering the question and what Obama means in the American landscape is to refer to Susan George's forceful arguments in the 2008 book, *Hijacking America: How the Religious and Secular Right Changed What Americans Think*. Here George asserts that since the seventies, not only has there been both secularly and religiously a general movement of American culture towards the right, but also that this belief system is so firmly entrenched that it is unlikely that one president (or a new party) can radically change it:

> This culture has been patiently constructed; it permeates the whole of American society from the leadership to the bottom rungs of the social ladder and it is not called into question because its assumptions are usually unspoken. They [the right] have nonetheless moved the center of gravity of American politics much further to the right (2).

Inversely, George contends that, as of 2008, "The Democratic Party no longer pretends that it is social-democratic or that it seeks to protect the poor and vulnerable. Anywhere but the United States, this party would be seen as a right-of-center organization, with many of its members en-

gaged in pushing the party further rightwards. Past or present 'conservative' European leaders like Angela Merkel or Jacques Chirac are probably
more progressive than most Democrats . . . " (5).

Though the book was published just before Obama's election to the
presidency, George's observations about a move to the right are useful
for a number of reasons:

1. As a sign of the times and of the pertinence of the theory we have
   studied, consider how George cites as European references for the
   Democratic Party in the United States a European Christian Democrat, Merkel, and a conservative (Chirac), whose party represents
   the interests of the Christian Democrats;
2. We have seen that there has been, as George argues, an undeniable
   progressive move to the right, where the relationship between
   church-state is considered in terms that, at least for the left, would
   have been unthinkable two decades ago. Works by Democrats
   such as Dionne's *Souled Out*, Dilulio's *Godly Republic*, and Jim Wallis's *The Great Awakening* and *Rediscovering Values* illustrate how the
   Democratic party has come to acknowledge the need for a greater
   role of religion in government while, at the same time, incorporat-
   ing religion into the progressive experience.[2] Moreover, within the
   public at large, the openness of the left to the role of religion can be
   seen when, in November, 2009, Democratic support for faith-based
   policy was at 77 percent—which was higher than with Republicans
   ("Faith-Based Programs Still Popular");
3. Beyond the observation of his being a pole of attraction for the
   Democratic liberal, the above considerations highlight how one
   may further evaluate the uniqueness and effectiveness of Obama's
   religious, "political left." In this respect, George's description of the
   Democratic Party applies at least in part to Obama in that he certainly does not represent its pre-seventies (or in other words six-
   ties) stance. However, condemning Obama as no longer being social-democratic because of this differentiation is subject to argument.

Mansfield touches on one argument when he asserts that Obama's
"fine words" in his famous 2004 speech[3] at the Democratic Convention
"were meant to echo the footsteps of nuns and clergymen who marched
with Martin Luther King Jr., of the religiously faithful who protested the
Vietnam War or helped build the labor movement or prayed with César
Châvez. Barack Obama was raising the banner of what he hopes will be
the faith-based politics of a new generation" (xv). At the same time, beyond the reference to a new generation and the 1960s, we have seen in
our study that Obama fits the definition of what David Osborne termed
in *Laboratories of Democracy*, a new paradigm politician. New paradigm
political theory holds that

a new paradigm emerges to replace a system that is becoming ineffective, or worse, detrimental to society . . . If a new paradigm is emerging, the traditional concepts of liberal and conservative may no longer apply. New paradigm politicians seek to step outside the established boundaries such as liberal and conservative to seek answers to problems caused by the dynamics of change. (Allen 159)

And Obama certainly did this when, as a post-Great Society liberal, he responded in his faith-based initiative to a policy which was pioneered by actors inspired directly or indirectly by what is essentially Christian-Democratic thought.

Overall, and inversely, Obama's "paradigmatic" faith policy also constitutes a response to an equally "paradigmatic" faith community that is radically challenging across the board the traditional perspectives concerning the role that religion should play in establishing social aid organizations and programs. Obviously, part of the equation of what constitutes the contemporary paradigmatic situation of the faith community is furnished by the move of the left to the right chronicled by George. But focusing uniquely on this trend in American culture is potentially limiting. Reciprocal to the move of the left to the right is also, as we have documented in this study, the religious right's embrace of the traditional leftist preoccupations with issues such as social justice.[4] And the faith-based story is only an indication of the scale of this appropriation. Borders are being erased and the trends we have been studying in the form of the faith-based story are only indicative of a wider appropriation of power that goes beyond the context of partnerships with government. In the case of evangelicals, for example, Nicolas Kristof highlights this new paradigm in social aid when he observes that:

For most of the last century, save-the-worlders were primarily Democrats and liberals. In contrast, many Republicans and religious conservatives denounced government aid programs.

Over the last decade, however, that divide has dissolved, in ways that many Americans haven't noticed or appreciated. Evangelicals have become the new internationalists, pushing successfully for new American programs against AIDS and malaria, and doing superb work on issues from human trafficking in India to mass rape in Congo. (11)

Kristof then adds that the largest U.S.-based international relief and development organization is Seattle-based, evangelical World Vision[5] "whose budget has roughly tripled over the last decade [and] now has 40,000 staff members in nearly 100 countries. That's more staff members than CARE, Save the Children and the worldwide operations of the United States Agency for International Development — combined" (11). And as is more commonly known, a legion of examples such as Katrina and more recently Joplin have lent high visibility to the role within the United States of faith-based organizations in general.

With these new concerns (encompassing environmental issues and world peace as well), new political affinities seem to be developing in many people traditionally considered as being on the religious right. In other words, a second move that is reciprocal to that of the left veering to the right is a potential openness to new political identification on the part of, for example, many traditionally conservative evangelicals. This was particularly apparent in the early stages of the 2008 election. Mansfield notes this phenomenon, specifying that evangelical support for Republican candidates had, by 2008, fallen from the 62 percent carried by Bush in the 2004 election to "a mere 29 per cent [who] were committed to Republican candidates" (xviii). Juxtaposed by many with the death or loss of influence of many of the Christian right's top leaders,[6] these results exemplify and concur with Dionne's evaluation that after the 2006 elections "there was a new religious landscape and that this new array of forces is more relevant to our future than were passed alignments. The results reflected the declining influence of the religious right, which [went] from being a major force in the majority coalition to acting as an irritant with a minority coalition" (19).[7] It is true that by the time of the actual election of 2008, white evangelical Protestants (as well as white Catholics) had aligned themselves within the contours of their more traditional support for the Republican Party. It is also true that Obama lost ground against both groups in the 2012 elections ("How the Faithful Voted"). Nonetheless, if the defection from Republican ranks did not become the widespread phenomenon that Mansfield suggested in 2008, it is the potential for it that should be underlined as a new and noteworthy trend in the American religious landscape. Particularly when we know that those evangelicals who have moved beyond the traditional confines of a conservative political agenda (dominated by questions such as homosexuality and abortion) are characterized by their youth.[8]

In general, then, even if the consensus within the American public of faith-based policy may be the result of, as George contends, the secular and religious right's triumph in changing the "way Americans think," Obama's policy concerning the role of government and religion may be seen as both a response to, and part of, a new paradigm situation where the traditional liberal and conservative perspectives are no longer applicable or effective. Obviously, in this blurring between left and right, Obama's attempt at creating a consensual, middle-of-the-road faith-based policy raises the question of what "the middle" means. And equally obvious, the debate about defining the "middle" (or center) is ongoing. However, if there are solid arguments[9] that America has taken an extreme turn to the right, the arguments of authors such as Dilulio and Alan Wolfe demonstrate that, at least in the context of our study of faith-based policy, Obama's approach may be considered a reasonable, moderate, and historically appropriate policy for the United States. Neither Dilulio nor Wolfe specifically mention Obama, but both offer analyses of

American history[10] in which Obama's pluralism and its expression in his policy may be seen as consistent with the intentions of the Founding Fathers. As such, the policy is a coherent extension of Obama's realistic and pragmatic view of faith in government and the consequent acknowledgment of what we have termed "efficiency in delivery" provided by faith-based organizations. Obama's policy, as well as Dilulio and Wolf's arguments, would seem therefore to reflect the subtext of Roger's *Claiming the Center* where the American "center" characterizes a moderate worldview that, tempered by an inherent respect for religious, cultural and political pluralism, is able at the same time to generate consensual policy which effectively betters the condition of the population as a whole.[11]

With the heritage of failed leadership left by the divisive Bush administration serving as a backdrop, it may thus be argued that the movement of the left to the right and the right to the left seemed to find a junction in the person and the faith-based policy of Barack Obama (at least in the early days of his presidency).[12] For an admirer like Mansfield, Obama seemed in the context of his person to synthesize with natural ease both the contemporary religious and political tendencies that would seem to be needed for effective leadership of the faith-based, government partnership. Mansfield notes that:

> Like his politics, [Obama's] life story is one that the public seems to embrace, and largely for its universal themes. In an unfathered, untethered generation, Obama often seems the Everyman in a heroic tale of spiritual seeking. Americans, as a people born of a religious vision, find in Obama at least a fellow traveller and at most a man at the vanguard of a new era of American spirituality. (xxi)

In general, Obama's attraction as an effective intermediary between church and state is to be found in his natural capacity to respond to the prevalent generational, political, religious and cultural realities, and paradigms of contemporary America.

More specifically in the context of the policy, for an admirer of Obama like Jim Wallis, "there hadn't been [before Obama] many good models recently, from either party, about how a White House should relate to religion and religious communities" (3). Wallis continues with the assertion that with Obama there is "an open door" (8) and a potential for an unprecedented relationship and partnership between government and the faith community (5). As Mansfield highlights the ways in which Obama's personality fits the age, so Wallis crystallizes the belief of many that on a larger scale the 2008 presidential election represented for the faith community "a milestone in [American] life and history" (4).

In sum, to meet the demands of the American people, Obama, synthesizes in the eyes of admirers like Mansfield and Wallis the requirements necessary to meet the challenges raised by the paradigmatic faith community and to be an effective leader of the faith-based, government partnership.[13] In reality, though, like so many other expectations that have been laid at the feet of Obama, those concerning his faith-based policy may be qualified as being, at the very least unrealistic, and at the very most, super-human.[14] This should not lead us, however, to underestimate Obama's work; if his policy is held by many to be imperfect and debatable, it may be considered nonetheless remarkable not simply because it is still "there," but also because it is thriving. And it is more than likely that no one else but Obama could have achieved what he has done. Whatever the case may be, my ultimate intention here is not to evaluate Obama as an unfulfilled Messiah, but rather to set off his on-going role as principal actor in the most contemporary chapter of the faith-based story. As such, he is part of a general effort emanating from a diverse group of actors who together constitute the hero of a story in American religiosity that most certainly will continue to unfold and be a litmus test for understanding the nation.

NOTES

1. In a 2010 interview, Rogers agreed that the middle-of-the-road reference had certainly become muddled in the Bush presidency (Personal interview 15 May 2010).

2. And as we have seen with Al Gore, political actors in the Democratic Party clearly began courting the religious vote before this millennium began. Although this strategy may be argued as intensifying in the election of 2004, it is rather misleading to assert that "the Democrats' eagerness to actively seek out the religious vote began with John Kerry's presidential campaign" (Pulliam "The Megachurch Primaries").

3. Obama specifically elicits the religious issue in the following passage: "The pundits like to slice-and-dice our country into Red States and Blue States; Red States for Republicans and Blue States for Democrats. But I've got news for them, too. We worship an awesome God in the Blue States" (*Dreams* 451).

4. A special case in this appropriation (in that it demonstrates the synthesis between left and right which seems to be occurring) can be found in the meteoric rise to power and influence of former misfit Jim Wallis. As Dan Gilgoff observes, in Wallis's more than thirty years in Washington, he has never been so popular: "As a politically progressive evangelical, he had long been an outcast in both evangelical and progressive political circles. Agitating for a greater government role in fighting poverty and promoting world peace, he pushed an agenda that was at odds with the Christian-right leaders who purported to speak for American evangelicals . . . Seemingly overnight, Wallis has gone from outside agitator . . . to inside player" ("Evangelical" 35). Wallis was named by Obama to serve on the first White House Advisory Council on Faith-based and Neighborhood Partnerships. In 1995, Wallis was instrumental in forming Call to Renewal, a national federation of churches, denominations, and faith-based organizations from across the theological and political spectrum working to overcome poverty. He is currently, with Mike Gerson, co-chairman of the Poverty Forum.

5. Mouw considers World Vision as an excellent illustration of alternative networking that, he asserts, is more efficient in delivering aid then that used by denominations or government agencies (Personal interview 22 Feb. 2010).

6. In his analysis of the 2008 presidential campaign, Mansfield observes that "the coalition of faith-based social conservatives that had defined the debate over religion in American politics for nearly three decades was in disarray, if not decline " (xvii).

This included the likes of Jerry Falwell, D. James Kennedy, Ted Haggard, and Pat Robertson.

7. For more detail concerning this movement, see Dionne, Chapter 2, "Why the Culture War Is the Wrong War: Religion, Values, and American Politics;" 45–70.

8. See, for example, Mansfield, ixx and xx. See, also, the poll, "Young White Evangelicals: Less Republican, Still Conservative." *The Pew Research, Religion and Public Life Project*. (The Pew Research Center. 28 Sept. 2007. Web. 21 Dec. 2007) http://www.pewforum.org/2007/09/28/young-white-evangelicals-less-republican-still-conservative/.

9. Such as George or Lynn.

10. Based on a study of the Framers perspectives concerning religion and government (and more generally, the American religious and political pluralist tradition), Dilulio's *Godly Republic* argues for a corrective in the interpretation of Church and State separation. Wolfe's *The Future of Liberalism* undertakes the demonstration of the historical inaccuracy behind the assumption that there is a tension between religion and liberalism in the United States.

11. Rogers agreed to this description of "the center" (Personal Interview 20 May 2013).

12. Wilson notes that "Democrats always avoided a progressive agenda. After the miserable failures of Gore and Kerry, progressives have argued that Democrats need to follow the conservative approach post-Goldwater and win by standing for something. Obama is trying to bridge these two approaches, to have integrity and progressive values, while simultaneously presenting a more centrist face that appeals across political boundaries" (125).

13. For Jim Wallis, Obama's person is the reflection in government of the coalition and the consensus that he has continually fought for in the faith community.

14. Jim Wallis explains that after writing his 2005 best-seller, *God's Politics*, in order to clarify the shortcomings that both the secular left and the religious right had in addressing the problem of social justice, he wrote his 2008 book, *The Great Awakening*, as a celebration of the unlimited possibility that, in large part, culminated with the arrival of Obama. Wallis advances that "A fundamental shift is taking place in America . . . A . . . new generation of the faithful is ending an age of narrow and divisive religion. This new faith coalition voted for a broad moral agenda for faith in public life. Racial and economic justice, peace-making and a more consistent ethical life will be the keystones of this growing shift" (1).

Works Cited

"About the Office of Faith-based and Neighborhood Partnerships." *whitehouse.gov*. Office of Faith-based and Neighborhood Partnerships. Web. 21 May 2011.

Allen, Charles, and Jonathan Portis. *The Comeback Kid: The Life and Times of Bill Clinton.* New York: Birch Lane, 1992. Print.

Bader, Christopher D., F. Carson Mencken and Paul Froese. "American Piety 2005: Content and Methods of the Baylor Religion Survey." Journal for the Scientific Study of Religion 46.4 (Dec. 2007): 447–64. Print.

Balz, Dan. "Partisan Polarization Intensified in 2004 Election, Only 59 of the Nation's 435 Congressional Districts Split Their Vote for President and House." *Washington Post* 29 Mar. 2005: A4. Print.

Bartkowski, John and Helen Regis. *Charitable Choices: Religion, Race, and Poverty in the Post- Welfare Era.* New York: New York University Press, 2001. Print.

Bellah Robert N. *Beyond Belief: Essays on Religion in a Post-Traditional World.* New York: Harper and Row, 1970. Print.

Benne, Robert. "Christians and Government." *The Oxford Handbook of Theological Ethics.* Eds. Gilbert Meilaender and William Werpehowski. Oxford: Oxford University Press, 2005. 325–42. Print.

Black, Amy, Douglas L. Koopman, and David K. Ryden. *Of Little Faith: The Politics of George W. Bush's Faith-Based Initiatives.* Washington D.C.: Georgetown University Press, 2004. Print.

"Black Churches and the Faith-Based Initiative: Findings from a Survey." *jointcenter.org*. Joint Center for Political and Economic Studies. Web. 17 June 2008. PDF file.

Brooks, David. "Obama, Gospel and Verse." *New York Times*. New York Times. Web. 20 Oct. 2007.

Bush, George. "Remarks by the President at the National Prayer Breakfast." Washington D.C. 1 Feb. 2001. Address. *whitehouse.gov*. The White House. Web. 10 June 2003.

———. "Commencement Address at the University of Notre Dame in Notre Dame, Indiana." *The American Presidency Project at the UC Santa Barbara.* University of California at Santa Barbara. Web. 10 June 2011.

———. "Executive Order 13199— Establishment of White House Office of Faith-Based and Community Initiatives." *The American Presidency Project at the UC Santa Barbara.* University of California at Santa Barbara. Web. 8 June 2011.

———. "The Duty of Hope Speech." *The Center for Public Justice.* The Center for Public Justice. Web. July 6 2002.

"Bush Pushes 'Faith-Based' Initiative during Meeting with Black Pastors." *Church and State* 58.3 (March 2005): 17. Print.

Butler, Jon. *Becoming America: the Revolution before 1776.* Cambridge: Harvard University Press, 2000. Print.

Carlson-Thies, Stanley. "Faith-based Initiative 2.0: The Bush Faith-based and Community Initiative." *Harvard Journal of Law and Public Policy*, 32.3 (Summer 2009): 931–47. Print.

———. Personal interview. 19 Feb. 2010.

———. Personal interview. 3 Aug. 2011.

———. Personal interview. 26 Oct. 2012.

———. "Re: "Comments." Message to John Chandler. 2 July 2013. E-mail.

Carlson-Thies, Stanley, and Dave Donaldson. *A Revolution of Compassion.* Grand Rapids: Baker Books, 2004. Print.

Casanova, José. *Public Religion in the Modern World*. Chicago: University of Chicago Press, 1994. Print

Clinton, Hillary. "Hillary Clinton on Supporting Faith-Based Institutions at the Ten Point National Leadership Foundation." *Berkley Center for Religion, Peace, and World Affairs*. Georgetown University. Web. 5 July 2011.

"CNN-USA Today-Gallup Poll: Majority Gives Bush Good Job Approval Mark." *cnn.com. CNN*. Web. 28 Dec. 2004.

Cohen, Patricia. "In Writings of Obama, a Philosophy Is Unearthed." *New York Times*. New York Times. Web. 21 June 2011.

Cochrane, Clarke E. "Life on the Border: A Catholic Perspective." *Church, State, and Public Justice: Five Views*. Ed. P.C. Kemeny. Downer's Grove: Inter Varsity Press, 2007: 39–66. Print.

Cone, James H. *A Black Theology of Liberation: Twentieth Anniversary Edition*: New York: Orbis, 1986. Print.

Connelly, Marjorie and Robin Toner. "Bush's Support on Major Issues Tumbles in Poll," *New York Times* 17 June 2005: A1. Print.

Dahl, Robert A. *Who Governs? Democracy and Power in an American City*. 2nd ed. New Haven: Yale University Press, 2005. Print.

Daly, Lew. *God and the Welfare State*. Cambridge Mass. & London, England: The MIT Press, 2006. Print.

———. *God's Economy: Faith-Based Initiatives and the Caring State*. Chicago: University of Chicago Press, 2009. Print.

Davis, Derek H. "Separation, Integration, and Accommodation: Religion and State in America in a Nutshell." *Church and State* 43.1 (Jan. 2001): 5–18. Print.

Dilulio Jr., John J. *Godly Republic: A Centrist Blueprint for America's Faith-based Future*. Berkeley: University of California Press, 2007. Print.

———. "Afterword: Why Judging Bush Is Never as Easy as It Seems." *Judging Bush*. Eds. Robert Maranto, Tom Lansford, and Jeremy Johnson. Stanford: Stanford University Press, 2009: 294–310. Print.

———. Personal interview. 21 Feb. 2010.

———. "Questions and Answers." christianitytoday.com. *Christianity Today*. Web. 25 May 2008.

———. "Re: New Developments concerning Faith-based Policy." Message to John Chandler. 26 Nov. 2012. E-mail.

Dilulio Jr., John J., and David Kuo. *"The Faith to Outlast Politics." New York Times*. New York Times. Web. 4 Feb. 2010.

Dionne Jr., E.J. *Souled Out: Reclaiming Faith and Politics after the Religious Right*. Princeton: Princeton University Press, 2008. Print.

Ehrenreich, Barbara. "The New Right Attack on Social Welfare." *The Mean Season: The Attack on the Welfare State*. Eds. Fred L. Block, Richard A. Cloward, Barbara Ehrenreich and Frances Fox Piven. New York: Pantheon Books, 1987: 161–96. Print.

"Faith-Based Programs Still Popular, Less Visible: Church-State Concerns Persist." *The Pew Forum on Religion and Public Life*. The Pew Research Center. Web. Dec. 11 2009.

Falsani, Cathleen. "I Have a Deep Faith." *Chicago Sun Times* 5 April 2005: A 2. Print.

Farnsley II, Arthur E. Book Review. "Faith-Based Politics: What Congregations Can and Can't Do." *The Christian Century* 24 Aug. 2004: 27–33. Print.

Fletcher, Michael. "Few Black Churches Get Funds: Small Percentage Participate in Bush's Faith-Based Initiative." *Washington Post* 19 Sept. 2006: A19. Print.

"Four More Years for the White House Office of Faith-based and Neighborhood Partnerships." *The Brookings Institution*. The Brookings Institution. Web. 4 Jan. 2013. PDF file.

Garner, Michelle D. "Advancing Discussion of Federal Faith-based Social Service Policies through Overview and Application of Established Health Services Research Models." *Advances in Social Work* 13.3 (Fall 2012): 484–509.

George, Susan. *Hijacking America: How the Religious and Secular Right Changed What Americans Think*. Cambridge, U.K.: Polity Press, 2009. Print.

Gergen, David. "Dueling for Values." *U.S. News and World Report* 23 May 2005: 58. Print.

Gerson, Michael, Personal interview. 12 May 2010.

Gingrich, Newt. *To Renew America*. New York: HarperCollins, 1995. Print.

Gilgoff, Dan. "Evangelical Minister Jim Wallis Is in Demand in Obama's Washington." *U.S. News and World Report*. 31 March 2009: 35. Print.

Goldberg, Michelle. *Kingdom Coming: The Rise of Christian Nationalism*. Rotterdam: Sense Publishers, 2011. Print.

Goldstein, Laurie, and David D. Kirkpatrick. "On a Christian Mission to the Top." *Class Matters. New York Times*. New York: Times Books, 2005: 73–86. Print.

Gore Jr., Albert A. "Speech Delivered to the Salvation Army." *The Center for Public Justice*. The Center for Public Justice. Web. 8 May 2009.

Grann, David. "Where We Got Compassion." *New York Times Magazine* 12 Sept. 1999: 62–65. Print.

Green, John C. "Winning Numbers." *The Christian Century* 30 Nov. 2004: 8. Print.

"Guidance For Government On The Design and Operation of a Constitutionally Valid 'Voucher'-Based Delivery System of Reentry Services for Ex-Offenders." *justice.gov*. United States Department of Justice. Web. 11 Dec. 2011.

Guidrais, Elisabeth. "Unequal America—Causes and Consequences of the Wide — and Growing — Gap between Rich and Poor." *Harvard Magazine* July-Aug. 2008: 22–29. Print.

Hall, Peter. *Inventing the Nonprofit Sector: Essays on Philanthropy, Voluntarism, and Nonprofit Organizations*. Baltimore: Johns Hopkins University Press, 1992. Print.

Hammack, David C. Rev. of *The Tragedy of American Compassion*, by Marvin Olasky. *Nonprofit and Voluntary Sector Quarterly* 25. (1996): 259–68. Print.

Holder, R. Ward and Peter B. Josephson. *The Irony of Barak Obama; Barack Obama, Reinhold Niebuhr, and the Problem of Christian Statecraft*. Farnham, U.K.: Ashgate Publishing Limited, 2012. Print.

"How the Faithful Voted." *Pew Research, Religion and Public Life Project*. The Pew Research Center. Web. 4 Dec. 2012.

Hunter, James Davison. *Culture Wars: The Struggle to Define America*. New York: Basic Books, 1991. Print.

Hutchinson Crocker, Ruth. *Social Work and Social Order: The Settlement Movement of Two Industrial Cities, 1889– 1930*. Urbana and Chicago, Illinois: Illinois University Press, 1992. Print.

"Initiatives: Faith-Based and Neighborhood Partnerships (FBNP)." *edgov*. The United States Department of Education. Web. 12 March 2012.

Javers, Eamon. "Obama Invokes Jesus More Often Than Bush: Obama Has Talked about His Religion in Several High-Profile Speeches." *cbsnews.com. CBS News*. Web. 19 May 2010.

Jellema, Dirk. "Abraham Kuyper's Attack on Liberalism." *The Review of Politics* 18.4 (Oct. 1957): 472–85. Print.

Jonas, Michael. "Sen. Clinton Urges Use of Faith-Based Initiatives." *Boston Globe* 1 Jan. 2005: A1. Print.

Keller, Bill, et al. *Class Matters*. New York: Times Books, 2005. Print.

Kemeny, P.C. Introduction. *Church, State and Public Justice: Five Views*. Ed. P.C. Kemeny. Downer's Grove: Inter Varsity Press, 2007. 11–37. Print.

King, Martin Luther. "I See the Promised Land." Memphis Tenn. 3 April 1963. Speech. *seto.org*. Web. 10 May 2011.

Kingston, Paul W. *The Classless Society*. Stanford: Stanford University Press, 2000. Print.

Kloppenberg, James T. *Reading Obama: Dreams Hope, and the American Political Tradition*. Princeton: Princeton University Press, 2011. Print.

Kristoff, Nicholas D. "Learning from the Sin of Sodom." *New York Times* 27 Feb. 2010: 11. Print.

Kuo, David. *Tempting Faith: An Inside Story of Political Seduction.* New York: Free Press, 2007. Print.

Leaming, Jeremy. "Loss of Faith: White House Faith Czar Towey Departs, as Doubts about Bush 'Faith-Based' Initiative Continue to Grow." *Church and State* 59.6 (June 2006): 16–19. Print.

Lebeaux, Charles, and Harold Wilensky. *Industrial Society and Social Welfare.* New York: Macmillan, 1965. Print.

Leonhardt, David. "Income Inequality." *New York Times.* New York Times. Web. 21 Dec. 2009.

Lynn, Barry. "Faith-based Procrastination: Religious Job Bias in Taxpayer-funded Program." *Washington Post.* Washington Post. Web. 27 Dec. 2012.

———. *Piety and Politics: The Right-wing Assault on Religious Freedom.* New York: Three Rivers Press, 2007. Print.

Mansfield, Stephen. *The Faith of Barack Obama.* Nashville: Thomas Nelson, 2008. Print.

"Majority Gives Bush Good Job Approval Mark." *CNN-USA Today-Gallup Poll.* CNN-USA Today. Web. 10 Feb. 2007.

McCarthy, Rockne M. and James W. Skilllen, Eds. *Political Order and the Plural Structure of Society.* Grand Rapids: Eerdmans, 1991. Print.

McKnight, Paul. "Five Streams of the Emerging Church—Key Elements of the Most Controversial and Misunderstood Movement in the Church Today." *Christianity Today* Feb. 2007: 37. Print.

Mills, C. Wright. *The Power Elite.* Oxford: Oxford University Press, 2000. Print.

Molotky, Daniel James. "Reinhold Niebuhr's Paradox: Groundwork for Social Responsibility." *Journal of Religious Ethics* 31 (March 2003): 101–23. Print.

Monsma, Stephen. *Positive Neutrality: Letting Religious Freedom Ring.* Westport, Conn.: Greenwood Press, 1993. Print.

———. *Putting Faith in Partnerships: Welfare-to-Work in Four Cities.* Ann Arbor: University of Michigan Press, 2004. Print.

Monsma, Stephen J. Christopher Soper. *The Challenge of Pluralism.* Lanham: Rowman and Littlefield, 2009. Print.

Moyers, Bill. "The Journal: Reverend Jeremiah Wright." *videopbs.org.* PBS. Web. 11 June 2011.

Mouw, Richard. *Abraham Kuyper: A Short and Personal Introduction.* Grand Rapids: Eerdmans, 2011. Print.

———. *The Challenges of Cultural Discipleship: Essays in the Line of Abraham Kuyper.* Grand Rapids: Eerdmans, 2012. Print.

———. Personal interview. 30 April 2008.

———. Personal interview. 22 February 2010.

———. Personal interview. 28 Oct. 2012.

Nathan, Richard. "Opening Remarks—The State of the Law: Legal Development Affecting Government Partnerships with Faith-Based Organizations: The Round Table on Religion and Social Welfare Policy." *The Pew Forum on Religion and Public Life.* The Pew Research Center. Web. 23 June 2011.

New York Times. *Class Matters.* New York: Times Books, 2005. Print

Nesbitt, Jim. "New Set of Emerging Values is Challenging Christian Conservatives." *The Presbyterian Outlook* 15 March 1999: 3–4, 9. Print.

Neuhaus, Richard John. *The Naked Public Square: Religion and Democracy in America.* Grand Rapids: Eerdmans, 1984. Print.

Nisbet, Robert A. *The Quest for Community: A Study in the Ethics of Order and Freedom.* Oxford: Oxford University Press, 1953. Print.

"Obama Announces White House Office of Faith-based and Neighborhood Partnerships." *whitehouse.gov.* The White House. Web. 10 March 2009.

Obama, Barack. "Amendments to Executive Order 13199 and Establishment of the President's Advisory Council for Faith-based and Neighborhood Partnerships." *whitehouse.gov.* The White House. Web. 12 Feb. Dec. 2009.

———. *The Audacity of Hope.* New York: Crown Publishers, 2006. Print.

———. *Dreams of My Father*. New York: Three Rivers Press, 1995. Print.

———. "Obama's 2006 Speech on Faith and Politics." *New York Times*. New York Times. Web. 27 Sept. 2006.

———. "President Obama at the National Prayer Breakfast." Washington D.C. 3 Feb. 2011. Address. *whitehouse.gov/blog*. The White House. Web. 15 March 2011.

"Obama's Favorite Theologian? A Short Course on Reinhold Niebuhr: Faith Angle Conference." *The Pew Forum on Religion and Public Life*. The Pew Research Center. Web. 16 June 2011.

Olasky, Marvin. *The Tragedy of American Compassion*. Washington D.C.: Regnery Publishing, 1992. Print.

———. *Compassionate Conservatism: What It Is, What It Does, and How It Can Transform America*. New York: The Free Press, 2000. Print.

Orr, John B. "Charitable Choice: A Primer for Faith-based Organizations." *USC Center for Religion and Civic Culture*. Univerisy of Southern California. Web. 3 March 2009.

Osborne, David. *Laboratories of Democracy*. Boston, Mass.: Harvard Business School Press, 1988. Print.

"Pew Forum on Religion and Public Life Releases First National Survey Probing Specifics of Support for Faith-Based Funding." *The Pew Forum on Religion and Public Life*. The Pew Research Center. Web. 12 Oct. 2002.

"Poll: Gloomy Economic Views; Bush Approval at New Low Thursday," *foxnews.com*. Fox News. Web. 6 May 2006.

Posner, Susan. "Obama's Faith-based Failure: A Troubling Hallmark of 'Compassionate Conservatism'—the Faith-based Initiative Persists despite Promises." *salon.com*. Web. 28 May 2012.

"Preserving Our Constitutional Commitments and Values." *whitehouse.gov*. Office of Faith-based and Neighborhood Partnerships. Web. 10 April 2009.

President's Advisory Council on Faith-Based and Neighborhood Partnerships. *A New Era of Partnerships: Report of Recommendations to the President*. *whitehouse.gov*. The White House. Web. 6 June 2010. PDF file.

"Promoting Interfaith Dialogue and Cooperation." *whitehouse.gov*. Office of Faith-based and Neighborhood Partnerships. Web. 21 May 2011.

"Promoting Responsible Fatherhood and Strong Communities." *whitehouse.gov*. Office of Faith-based and Neighborhood Partnerships. Web. 19 May 2011.

"Protecting the Civil Rights and Religious Liberty of Faith-Based Organizations: Why Religious Hiring Rights Must Be Preserved." *whitehouse.gov*. The White House. Web. 12 Dec. 2005. Pdf file.

Pulliam, Sarah. "The Megachurch Primaries: How the leading Democratic Candidates Are Trying to Win Evangelical Votes." *ctlibray.com*. Christianity Today. Web. 10 March 2008. Print.

———. "The Perfect Hybrid," *Christianity Today* (May, 2009): 46–50.

"Reducing Unintended Pregnancies, Supporting Maternal and Child Health, and Reducing the Need for Abortion." *whitehouse.gov*. Office of Faith-based and Neighborhood Partnerships. Web. 16 May 2011.

Reed Jr., Adolph. "The 2004 Election in Perspective: The Myth of 'Cultural Divide' and the Triumph of Neo-liberal Ideology." *American Quarterly* 52.2 (March, 2005): 1–25. Print.

Rogers, Jack. *Claiming the Center: Churches and Conflicting Worldviews*. Louisville: Westminster John Knox Press, 1995. Print.

———. Personal interview. 3 May 2008.

———. Personal interview. 15 May 2010.

———. Personal interview. 20 May 2013.

Schlesingler Jr., Arthur. "Forgetting Reinhold Niebuhr." *New York Times*. New York Times. Web. 7 May 2011.

Scott, Janny, and David Leohardt. "Shadowy Lies the still Divide." *Class Matters*. New York: Times Books, 2005. 1–26. Print.

Silk, Mark. "Faith-based Executive Order Finally off the Ground." *Religious News Service*. University of Missouri. Web. 12 June 2012.

Skillen, James. "What Distinguishes the Center for Public Justice?" *The Center for Public Justice*. The Center for Public Justice. Web. 21 June 2010.

Skowronek, Stephen. "The Conservative Insurgency and Presidential Power: A Developmental Perspective on the Unitary Executive." *Harvard Law Review* 122.8 (2009): 2070–103. Print.

Smidt, Corwin. "Principled Pluralist Response." *Church, State and Public Justice: Five Views*. Ed. P.C. Kemeny. Downers Grove: InterVarsity Press, 2007. 72–73. Print.

———. "The Principled Pluralist Perspective." *Church, State and Public Justice: Five Views*. Ed. P.C. Kemeny. Downers Grove: InterVarsity Press, 2007. 127–61. Print.

Spykman, Gordon. "Sphere sovereignty in Calvin and the Calvinist Tradition." *Exploring the Heritage of John Calvin*. Ed. David E Holwera. Grand Rapids: Baker, 1976: 163–208. Print.

"Strengthening the Role of Community in the Economic Recovery." *whitehouse.gov*. Office of Faith-based and Neighborhood Partnerships. Web. 16 May 2011.

"Ten Most Important Obama Faith Moments." *usnews.com*. U.S. News and World Report. Web. 22 May 2010.

Thiemann, Ronald. *Religion in Public Life: A Dilemma for Democracy*. Washington, D.C.: Georgetown University Press, 1996. Print.

Tillich, Paul. *The Courage to Be*. 2nd ed. New Haven: Yale University, 2000. Print.

"Towey Leaving Helm of Faith-Based Initiatives." *The Christian Century* 16 May 2006: 14. Print.

Tuttle, Robert W. "The State of the Law: Legal Development Affecting Government Partnerships with Faith-Based Organizations." *The Round Table on Religion and Social Welfare Policy*. The Rockefeller Institute of Government. Web. 23 June 2011.

"U.S. Religious Landscape Survey." *The Pew Forum on Religion and Public Life*. The Pew Research Center. Web. 30 Dec. 2009.

Van Til, Kent A. *Calvin Theological Journal*. 40 (2005): 267–289. Print.

Wallis, Jim. *The Great Awakening: Seven Ways to Change the World—Reviving Faith and Politics*. New York: HarperCollins, 2008. Print.

———. *God's Politics*. New York: HarperCollins, 2005. Print.

———. *Rediscovering Values: On Wall Street, Main Street and Your Street*. New York: Howard Books, 2010. Print.

Waters, David. "Obama's faith-based inertia." *The Washington Post* 9 Feb. 2010: 9, 25. Print.

Wentz, Richard. *Religion in the New World—The Shaping of Religious Traditions in the United States*. Minneapolis: Fortress Press, 1990. Print.

"White House Releases Final Faith-based Panel Names." *The Christian Century* 5 May 2009: 18. Print.

White, John Kenneth. *The New Politics of Old Values*. Hanover and London: University Press of New England: 1988. Print.

Wills, Garry. *Head and Heart*. New York: Penguin Press: 2007. Print.

Wilson, John K. *Barack Obama: This Improbable Quest*. Boulder: Paradigm Publishers, 2008. Print.

Witham, Larry. "100–Year-Old Idea Inspires Proposals to Revamp Welfare: Pluralism Offers Role for Religion." *The Washington Times* 3 Jan. 1996: A 2. Print.

Wolin, Sheldon S. *Managed Democracy and the Specter of Inverted Totalitarianism*. Princeton: Princeton University Press, 2008. Print.

Wolfe, Alan. *The Future of Liberalism*. New York: Vintage Books, 2009. Print.

Zeleny, Jeff and Brian Knowlton. "Obama Wants to Expand Role of Religious Groups." *New York Times*. New York Times. Web. 10 Sept. 2011.

Zuckerman, Mortimer B. "A Closer Look at America." *U.S. News and World Report* 13 Dec. 2004: 68. Print.

Index

About the Author

John Chandler earned his master's in philosophy and his doctorate from the University of Paris–Sorbonne. He is senior lecturer at the *Université de Valenciennes* in France, where he teaches American Cultural Studies. He has published widely on social aid policy and religion in the United States.

CPSIA information can be obtained at www.ICGtesting.com
Printed in the USA
BVOW02*2253081213

338486BV00002B/3/P